Franklin Sherman
April, 1952

PS

CHRISTIANITY AFTER FREUD

CHRISTIANITY AFTER FREUD

*An Interpretation of the
Christian Experience in the
light of Psycho-Analytic Theory*

by
B. G. SANDERS, M.A.

LONDON

GEOFFREY BLES

Printed in Great Britain by
Butler & Tanner Ltd., Frome and London
for Geoffrey Bles Ltd.
52 Doughty Street, London, W.C.1
First Published 1949

TO
MY BROTHER

CONTENTS

THE UNIVERSAL NEUROSIS AND THE DIVINE PSYCHIATRY

8

PREFACE

THIS essay was written with a single object in view, which may perhaps best be explained by giving a brief account of its origin.

Some years ago I read with deep interest and fascination Freud's book *Moses and Monotheism*, and it is to that that I can now trace the conception of this essay. About the same time, in the summer of 1941, I also read Frazer's *Golden Bough* and Robertson Smith's *Religion of the Semites*, and I was presented with the problem of reconciling my beliefs as a Christian with the discoveries and theories of Comparative Religion and Psycho-analysis, but particularly with the latter.

I then endeavoured, by reading Freud's works more systematically, to come to a solution of my problem, and to gain a fuller understanding of Psycho-analysis; and it was while thus engaged that the thought struck me, which is the real basis of this essay, that Freud's view of Religion depends solely upon the presupposition that God does not exist. This presupposition, however, was not stated; but the conclusions of the argument were presented as resulting from the use of the Psycho-analytic method. As a Christian, who so far as I could judge was persuaded of the validity of this Psycho-analytic method, I was thus in a difficult situation. I could not deny the truth of the presupposition that God does exist and is the source of all existence, and I could not deny that, although perhaps in its infancy, Psycho-analysis was a valid scientific method. This essay is not, however, a compromise between these two beliefs, but rather, as it appears to me, the only way in which my religious and scientific views can be reconciled. Before going further, therefore, there are two points which should be noticed carefully. First, if my view of Psycho-analysis is wrong, then what I have attempted to do in this essay is unnecessary. Second, if my view of Religion is wrong, then from another point of view, it is equally un-necessary. And I would emphasize this strongly, as I realize that there are many who will incline to one or other of these two positions. But if we are prepared to accept the Psycho-analytic method as valid, and also to believe in the existence of God and the truth of the Christian Religion, then we must also be prepared to subject the Christian Faith to Psycho-analytic examination. This is all that I have tried to do here: to examine, and therefore also to interpret, the Christian Religion from a Psycho-analytic point of view, and to show how, with the presupposition that God exists—a presupposition which Natural Science can neither prove nor disprove—Christianity remains a reasonable faith.

This essay is all through an *argumentum ad hominem*, and therefore accepts for the sake of the argument much that some readers, both Christians and Psycho-analysts, may not be willing to agree with; and this raises the question whether or not the method of argument which I have adopted is a sound one. In answer to this, I would say that there are two ways, and two ways only, in which it is possible to treat Psycho-analysis. As it is a scientific system of which each part depends upon each preceding part, it does not seem to me to be legitimate to accept the parts of it which we like, and to reject those we do not like. Thus, for example, it would be illegitimate to accept Freud's theories about the unconscious or about repression, and to reject his ideas about the Œdipus complex or infantile sexuality. The system is a whole, and must therefore be accepted as a whole, or rejected as a whole. To my mind these are the only two ways of dealing with Psycho-analysis as a scientific method. The same is also true of the Christian Religion. We cannot accept one part of it and reject others: we cannot, for example, remain Christians by accepting Jesus' moral teaching, if we are going to reject belief in his true divinity. From the Annunciation to the Ascension the life of Jesus forms one whole, out of which we cannot pick and choose.

Now some Christians have rejected Psycho-analysis wholly, and have given good grounds for doing so. But if we cannot agree with their arguments, or, rather, as the Psycho-analyst will not agree with them, then the task of the defender of religious faith must be to use Psycho-analysis, without distorting it, to interpret and explain his religion. He must endeavour as it were to translate his religion into the new language; and that is all that I have tried to do in this essay. I would therefore repeat that if Psycho-analysis is illogical and untrustworthy as a scientific method, then such an essay as this is unnecessary: but if it is not, then I believe that this is, in principle at any rate, the only logical and legitimate way of dealing with its apparent threat to religious belief.

Wherein, then, does this threat lie? Until recent years Psycho-analysis as a method of psychotherapy only found support within a comparatively small and almost exclusively medical circle, while it was received by the majority with indifference, suspicion, or hostility, which seemed appropriate to what was regarded as a new-fangled and untrustworthy pseudo-science. It was not long, however, before Psycho-analysis became more than just a clinical method of treating certain types of nervous disorders, in which field even its enemies could not deny it some success. Sigmund Freud, the real originator of Psycho-analysis, and his disciples, soon began to apply the Psycho-analytic method to the examination of subjects far removed from the physician's consulting room, and in particular to the investigation of what Freud has himself called the "universal obsessional neurosis" [1]—Religion. Much of Freud's writing seems to strike at the very foundations of the Christian belief in God.

Furthermore, this hostility is not merely one-sided. Religion may recognize an opponent in Psycho-analytical Science, but Freudianism also recognizes its own chief opponent in Religion. Thus Freud himself says that "of the three forces which can dispute the position of Science, religion alone is a really serious enemy".[2]

The challenge thus presented to Christianity is not one that can be lightly disregarded, since Freud's arguments are very plausible, and if it goes unanswered the Freudian theory may prove in the long run to be a formidable power in

[1] *The Future of an Illusion*, p. 76.
[2] *New Introductory Lectures on Psycho-Analysis*, p. 205.

turning men further away from God. In the present age what passes popularly under the name of Psychology has been presented to the public as a kind of universal remedy for the mental, material, and moral ills of civilization. One need only look at the average cheap bookstall to realize what a flood of such pseudo-psychological literature is on the market, offering to modern man the modern equivalent of the Gospel of Salvation. Indeed, much of this that purports to be Psychology may be a rather untrustworthy guide to the subject, if not actually a misrepresentation of it; but behind it all one may see the growing influence of what the Christian may well call the new Gnosis.

This essay, as I have already indicated, has a single aim: namely, to reconcile what I believe to be two views of life which are only apparently hostile to one another. The real opponent of Religion is not so much the Scientific method, as the presuppositions according to which that method is employed. This essay is divided, therefore, into three parts, the first of which is devoted to a general defence of Religious Faith in face of the theories brought against it by Psycho-analytic research, and to an attempt to show that the conclusion of the argument of each side rests upon, and is determined by, the presupposition concerning the nature of God which that side adopted either implicitly or explicitly at the outset. This will necessitate a short restatement of the Christian view of man's relations with God, in order to show the reasonableness of Religion, if one is willing to accept in the first place belief in the existence of God, and in the second the validity of the Psycho-analytic method of investigation. In the second and third parts, which are in a sense extended appendices to the first, we are led to a fuller treatment of the two great facts in human history—the origin of sin, and the way of man's salvation—in the light of Psycho-analytic research into the nature and behaviour of the human mind. Here I would say that the conclusions to which this restatement of the Christian experience in the terms of Psycho-analysis brings us, need cause neither surprise nor alarm, for this is not the first time that a Christian apologist has had to restate his faith in such a manner. In fact, the demands of apologetic and the changing language and thought of successive centuries make such a course inevitable, as may be seen from the writings of the Early Fathers of the Christian Church, who constantly endeavoured to reinterpret the Christian Faith in the language and thought used by, and acceptable to, their heathen and heretical contemporaries—a process which also enabled them and their successors to understand more fully the mysteries of the Faith. I would, therefore, emphasize once more, that this essay is intended primarily as an *argumentum ad hominem*, and not as a statement of absolute and universal validity; that it does not attempt any philosophical justification of the presuppositions on which the Christian faith is based; and that in it I have endeavoured only to interpret, and not to add to, nor subtract from, the Christian Gospel.

The whole is presented in the hope and belief that it may perhaps help in this present age to make the eternal truths of the Christian Faith better understood by the faithful and more readily acceptable to those for whom Religion means little or nothing. One cannot hope even by the most logical argument to convince those who at the outset are unwilling to believe in and to worship God; but if this may prove of any help to the faithful or the doubtful, its purpose will indeed have been accomplished.

BELIEF IN GOD AND THE PSYCHO-ANALYTIC METHOD

1. *The Challenge of Psycho-analysis*

IN the concluding chapter of a book published some twenty-two years ago,[1] Professor Clement C. J. Webb wrote as follows:

> A contrast especially notable to those interested in the general subject to the consideration of which this volume is devoted is that between the attitude to scientific views which challenged Christian tradition adopted by Christian Theologians half a century ago, and that of their successors today. No such outcry as that with which the theories of Darwin were received has been aroused by those of Freud, although the latter might well seem fraught with far more danger to the ordinary Christian's religious life than the former. On the contrary, the reception accorded by the religious world to the speculations of the psycho-analysts is chargeable rather with undue precipitation than with excessive suspicion or distrust.

Many may wonder how it is that Psycho-analysis, which originated simply as a clinical method for the treatment of mental disorders, has become such a menace to the Christian Faith. The answer to this may perhaps best be provided by the originator of Psycho-analysis himself. In the preface to Theodor Reik's book *Ritual* (p. 5), Professor Freud writes as follows:

> Psycho-analysis was born of medical necessity . . . its further progress led away from the study of the physical conditions of nervous illnesses in a degree surprising to the physician, and gradually the whole mental content of human life came within its sphere, including the healthy—the normal as well as the super-normal.

This in itself is both reasonable and harmless enough from

[1] *Science, Religion and Reality*, p. 341.

15

the Christian point of view; but when the results of such an all-pervading application of Psycho-analysis are perceived, the danger of this new Science is more apparent. Later, in the same Preface, for example, Freud says:

> If we submit the prehistoric and ethnological material relating to this archaic heritage (i.e. the Œdipus complex) to psychoanalytical elaboration we come to an unexpectedly definite conclusion—namely, that god the father at one time walked incarnate on the earth and exercised his sovereignty as leader of the hordes of primitive men, until his sons combined together and slew him; and further, that the first social ties, the basic moral restrictions, and the oldest form of religion—totemism—originated as a result of, and a reaction against, this liberating misdeed.[1]

Again, in *Moses and Monotheism*, he writes:

> From then (1912) on I have never doubted that religious phenomena are to be understood only on the model of the neurotic symptoms of the individual, which are so familiar to us, as a return of long-forgotten important happenings in the primeval history of the human family, that they owe their obsessive character to that very origin, and therefore derive their effect on mankind from the historical truth they contain (p. 94).

It is in the use made of such hypotheses as these that the threat to the Christian Religion lies. By subjecting the material supplied by the comparative study of religions to Psycho-analytical examination, Psycho-analysts have made a very plausible attempt to demolish the foundations upon which Christianity is built. This is done first by drawing the seemingly logical conclusion from the works of such students of Comparative Religion as Frazer and Robertson Smith, that Christianity belongs to the same class as all other religions, and secondly by making the assertion that heathen religion has its origin in the human mind alone and from purely temporal causes, in the same way as the obsessive symptoms of neurotics, and so concluding that the idea of God is nothing more than a projection of man's own unconscious desires and fears. Thus, Freud's disciple, Reik, can write

Ritual, p. 9.

with absolute confidence: "Psycho-analysis has proved that the idea of God in the life of the individual and of the people has its origin in the veneration and exaltation of the father," [1] and again: "Religion itself, however, as we know, is a creation of mental functions born under the pressure of mental forces." [2] Such quotations as these make it clear that the Christian must take Psycho-analysis seriously if he is going to answer effectively this challenge which it offers to his Faith; and in the light of recent experience he may well wonder how best he is going to counter its attacks.

2. *Comparison with the Challenge of Natural Science*

In the last century the development of the study of Natural Science and particularly the publication of Darwin's *Origin of Species* revealed a serious adversary to the Christian Church. Now after a long period of controversy the state of affairs existing between the two parties grouped under the respective standards of Science and Religion has settled into an uneasy truce, in which both sides would claim a victory, although neither seems certain in its own mind that the other has been defeated. Scientifically-minded Churchmen and religious Scientists do periodically make efforts to reconcile the two adversaries, but unfortunately their work is hampered, since the would-be peacemakers do not seem to realize that not only has the struggle gone on too long for the opponents to be reconciled by a few carefully chosen words, but also that the real disagreement between Religion and Science rests upon a difference of fundamental principles which logical argument alone cannot resolve. The two parties, perhaps without realizing it, rest their cases upon contrary and irreconcilable presuppositions—Religion upon belief in God, and in the complete dependence of man upon him: Science upon belief in Man, and in human self-sufficiency. Neither of these beliefs can, it would appear, be absolutely proved or disproved by rational arguments to the satisfaction of both parties, and so it has come about that, while there are many who do

[1] Ibid., p. 73. [2] Ibid., p. 22.

not realize the present incompatibility of the two Philosophies, the Scientific and the Religious, the two parties now stand apart, each more or less indifferent to the other's existence, but each claiming that its own position is the more rational.

While now, however, the two causes are thus in a sense irreconcilable, it is, I think, true that in the beginning of the controversy they need not have been so, had it not been for the excesses of zealots on both sides; for Natural Science was not in origin at any rate bound to a non-theistic philosophy of life. In particular we should regret that attitude of mind among certain ecclesiastics, who, misunderstanding the real meaning of the inspiration of Holy Scripture, endeavoured to uphold the truth of Religion by going to fantastic lengths to deny the demonstrable facts discovered by students of Natural Science. A similar thing had already happened in the time of Galileo, although later the Church had the good sense to acknowledge the truth of the scientific discoveries which it had previously condemned as heresy. Thus at the outset great bitterness was engendered against the Church by the perverse and ill-founded criticism of Natural Science from the lips of those who represented Religion, whose fault was merely that they did not grant to Science that autonomy in its own sphere which was its due, with the inevitable result that Science entered the sphere which really belonged to Theology not as an ally but as an invader, and was then forced to set up what proved to be an atheistic Religion of its own.

Here, however, we are not concerned with going over the old ground of the Science-Religion controversy. This brief and perhaps inadequate résumé of the great controversy of the last century is only given here, so that in facing a new challenge to Christianity we may have it before us as a warning, lest we fall into errors similar to those of our predecessors.

3. *Presuppositions and the Psycho-analytic Method*

The arguments of the Psycho-analyst on the subject of the Christian Religion depend, as has been indicated above, on theories derived from two different sources: first, on the validity of the comparison of Christianity with heathen religions, and second on the claim that, like a neurosis, heathen religion has its origin solely in the human mind. These theories, however, are not in themselves anti-religious, and, if based upon Christian presuppositions, may be used in demonstration of the reasonableness of Christianity. The Christian cannot deny the real meaning of heathen worship, although he may be fully aware of its inadequacy, unless he is prepared to deny also the truth of the findings of the comparative study of Religion; nor can he deny that God works in man through the human mind. In other words, the use of such arguments against religion depends not so much on the arguments themselves, as on the presuppositions of the arguer. In fact, I believe that the theory which Freud has constructed to explain away religious belief is only anti-religious so long as it rests upon the presupposition that there is no God, which is, of course, the conclusion that the argument is intended to prove. If this belief is correct, then this is an entirely illogical process, for it is a circular argument—a kind of ontological argument for the non-existence of God, rejecting belief in God, because the idea of God appears to be impossible to the human intelligence.

The real difference, therefore, between the Psychoanalytic view of Religion and the Christian arises, I would suggest, from a difference of absolute presuppositions, which depend in the last resort on an ultimate difference of the will —to believe in God or not to believe in God. In brief, it is nothing more nor less than a renewal, under fresh colours and with more novel armament, of the age-old controversy between belief in God and belief in no God; and when we say, "I believe in God", it should be noticed that this is primarily an act of the will, "I am willing to acknowledge the existence of, and my own dependence on, God", and not of the intellect, "I agree with the proposition that there is a God". The former is truly a religious statement, the latter a philosophical statement; and our concern here is with Religion rather than Philosophy. If, however, it were merely a question of absolute presuppositions, the argument would be at an end, an impasse not to be removed by further discussion. But it is constantly claimed by Freud and his followers, implicitly if not actually explicitly, that it is the Pscyho-analytic method of investigation that proves the theories of Psycho-analysis on the origin and nature of Religion; no mention is made of absolute presuppositions. If, therefore, such a claim is well founded, and the argument does not depend on presuppositions, then it ought to be possible to examine the origins of Religion by the Psycho-analytic method and with the presupposition that God exists, and still to come to the conclusion that belief in the existence of God is merely a projection of human desires or fears, a product of the human mind alone. This, however, we shall not find; but we shall undoubtedly come back to the point from which we started—to the conclusion, which began as a presupposition, that God exists; for all argument depends upon some presupposition, whether it is stated or not, and this conditions the end to which the argument must lead. And so when in the course of the argument we seem to be forced back to the human mind as the original source of belief in God, we shall, unless we abandon our primary presupposition, still have the God, whose existence we presupposed, as the ultimate cause of what may otherwise have appeared to be a purely human creation; belief in God will be there all the time. Such an argument will in one sense prove nothing, for it will itself be a circular argument; but it will at least show that the Psycho-analytic *method* by itself proves nothing against Religion, but may be used as well to defend belief in God as to attack it. If, therefore, we base our argument on an absolute presupposition, and the conclusion corresponds with that presupposition, it will, it is true, be a circular argument, but it will also at least justify our belief that the conclusion of the Freudian theory also depends on a circular argument and starts from an absolute presupposition. With this limited intention in view I intend to embark upon a sympathetic examination of Religion by Psycho-analytic methods, and so to see if the hypothesis is true that has been set out previously, that the presuppositions of the theorist determine the conclusions of his argument.

4. *The Proper Scope of Psycho-analysis*

It is at this point that we should recall what may now be seen to have been the errors of those who in the last century tried to defend Religion against the attacks of the Natural Scientists. In that unhappy controversy, as we have already observed, Science was not allowed an intellectual autonomy in its own sphere, which is the examination of cause and effect in the natural order. While granting to Natural Science the right to pursue its task of examining cause and effect in this way, the limitations of Science must not be forgotten—namely, that, when it appears to have discovered the cause of some natural phenomenon, it has not reached an absolute end, but has merely put the field of research a stage further back. Writing on the work of Charles Darwin, the late Sir Arthur Shipley said:

> No body of scientific doctrine succeeds in describing in terms of laws of succession more than some limited set of stages of a natural process; the whole process—if indeed it can be regarded as a whole—must for ever be beyond the reach of scientific grasp. The earliest stage to which Science has succeeded in tracing back any part of a sequence of phenomena itself constitutes a new problem for Science and that without end. There is always an earlier stage and to an earliest we can never attain. The questions of origins concern the theologian, the metaphysician, perhaps the poet.[1]

Even, however, within these limitations it remains the task and the right of Science to explore and to continue exploring, and Christians would be ill advised to deny to Science the authority to do so, or to limit that authority to certain approved fields of research, as if they were afraid of what Science might discover. Nevertheless it is not the right of Natural Science to make absolute presuppositions, whether

[1] Reprinted in *Cambridge Cameos*, pp. 140–1.

positive or negative; all scientific theories must be based upon scientific data, not on speculation, or such theories will cease to be scientific.

Modern defenders of the Christian Faith are perhaps more willing than their predecessors to allow such a proper authority to Natural Science. They are, for example, no longer concerned to defend by fallacious proofs myths, such as the story of Adam and Eve in the Garden of Eden, as historical truths. With this warning in our minds, we shall endeavour in our examination of Religion, to face Psycho-analysis on its own ground, and to concede to it authority in its own sphere, which is the study of the nature and behaviour of the human mind. In the following argument we shall accept the Psycho-analytic method as valid, and the discoveries of Psycho-analytic investigation into psychical activity as authoritative so far as they concern, and are confined to, the working of the human mind. This means that we cannot accept without qualification the purely speculative theories which are alleged to be based on the investigation of neurotic obsessions and savage religious institutions, since these theories appear to depend, as has been suggested, not on positive research, but on preconceived ideas. I would here remind readers of something written by C. S. Lewis, which expresses perfectly the scope and limitations of Psycho-analysis.

Now you want to distinguish very clearly between two things: between the actual medical theories and technique of the psycho-analysts, and the general philosophical view of the world which Freud and some others have gone on to add to this. The second thing—the philosophy of Freud—is in direct contradiction to Christianity, and also in direct contradiction to the other great psychologist, Jung. And furthermore, when Freud is talking about how to cure neurotics he is speaking as a specialist on his own subject; but when he goes on to talk general philosophy he is speaking as an amateur. It is therefore quite sensible to attend to him with respect in the one case and not in the other—and that's what I do.[1]

[1] *Christian Behaviour*, p. 21.

Furthermore, as the Psycho-analytic theory of the origin of religion depends for its material largely on the findings of the comparative study of religion, we too shall accept their findings as authoritative, so long as they are strictly concerned with the comparison and interpretation of ancient and modern heathen religions. We shall thus be able to start our argument from the same premiss as the Psycho-analyst—that Christianity and heathen religion are fundamentally of the same nature—while realizing, of course, the ineffectiveness of heathenism, and that it is on a generally lower plane both morally and philosophically. As the argument develops we may have to revise this rather simple view, but for the present we will accept their apparent general similarity. This similarity need not alarm modern Christians, for it was realized, and used as a basis for evangelism, in the primitive Church.[1]

5. *The Presuppositions of Religious Belief*

The fundamental presupposition of all religion, whether Christian or heathen, is belief in God, even though such belief may not be codified or set down in any creeds or dogmatic formulæ. By the word "God" we mean a personal supernatural power, whose existence is accepted as a matter not of knowledge, but of faith. To such a God the religious man, be he savage or civilized, believes that he owes a sort of allegiance or worship based upon ambivalent feelings of attraction and repulsion. As Otto has said:

> The dæmonic-divine object may appear to the mind an object of horror and dread, but at the same time it is no less something that allures with a potent charm, and the creature, who trembles before it, utterly cowed and cast down, has always at the same time the impulse to turn to it, nay even to make it somehow his own.[2]

---

[1] Compare Acts, xvii, 23. "For as I passed by, and beheld your devotions, I found an altar with this inscription, TO THE UNKNOWN GOD. Whom therefore ye ignorantly worship, him declare I unto you."

[2] *The Idea of the Holy*, p. 31.

This idea of God, which underlies all real religion, is to be distinguished from what we shall call, for convenience, the Deity of the Philosopher. Such a Deity is completely different from a God who is worshipped by the faithful, for its existence is not a matter of faith, but the result of a logical deduction. It is important to notice this difference, for in spite of the fact that Christian philosophers have endeavoured to prove the existence of God by reason, and in spite of superficial similarities between the two ideas of the Creator, the Deity of the philosopher is not necessarily a personal being, nor an object to whom worship is owed as a direct result of belief in its existence: and it is not with such a rational idea of God, but with apparently irrational belief, that Psycho-analysis is primarily concerned, although, indeed, Psycho-analytic arguments may be produced to explain why men should produce rational arguments for the existence of what they may call God as the originator of the universe. Of course, it should also be remembered that similar arguments could be produced to explain belief in the non-existence of God. However, the distinction between the Religious and the Philosophical view of God is, I believe, a real one, even though it may appear somewhat arbitrary, and though sometimes it may be difficult to place a particular system in one class or the other. This is due to the influence which religion undoubtedly has upon philosophy, and to the necessity of formulating religious belief in philosophical terms. Here then we are not concerned with any religions which, depending on ideas of God founded on rational arguments, are not so much Religious in the strict sense as Philosophical systems. For our purpose, Religion may be defined as rather an emotional than an intellectual view of life.

Further in Hebrew Religion, and also in its successor Christianity, God is believed to reveal himself, or to be revealed, in human history; that is, God is made known to men through his actions in the world and through the lives and works of human beings, as well as through his activity in maintaining and directing the orderly progress of the natural order. In particular the Jews believed that God revealed his

24

purpose and his nature to them through his treatment of them as his chosen people, as that purpose and nature were interpreted through the mouths of the great leaders of Israel. Especially was this true of Moses and the prophets, and to their names Christianity has added the name of Jesus of Nazareth through whose life and teaching God has given a revelation of himself which is claimed to be both complete and final.

Moreover, both Hebrew and Christian religions maintain not only that God created and set in order the whole of the universe in which we live, but also that within the framework of that creation man was created with an appointed purpose to fulfil here on earth. In order to achieve this, man was created, unlike the rest of God's animal creation, in the image and likeness of God, that is, with a mind capable of rational thought, and with a capacity for worship and for moral behaviour which imply an ability to discriminate, and a freedom to choose, between right and wrong. Man, having at first been created without sin, fell into sin through a misuse of his power of free will, which consequently was automatically limited through his bondage to sin. In this connection it may be convenient to notice the fact that Christian Theology has never been able to come to an agreed decision on the freedom of the will in fallen man: for, while the most ardent supporter of free will may feel a certain compulsion in some of the acts which he believes he performs of his own free choice, the determinist also cannot wholly give up the idea that even he has some degree of control over his actions. It is important to realize this, and therefore also to realize that the apparent determinism, almost the pessimistic fatalism, attributed to Psycho-analysis is not necessarily in conflict with Christian thought, and may not therefore be adduced as proof of the error of Psycho-analysis. For, though it may be said that Psycho-analysis can neither prove nor disprove determinism, the same may also be said of Christian Theology.[1]

All the beliefs of both Hebrew Religion and Christianity

[1] Compare *Science, Religion and Reality*, p. 318.

depend on the fundamental presupposition of belief in the existence of God, and have arisen from the further development and expansion of this presupposition in the light of human experience. Conversely, the peculiar doctrines of Hebrew and Christian Religion stand or fall according to the truth of this belief in the existence of God.

6. *The Development of Religion*

If we subject the origins of the Hebrew Religion to a close examination, we shall find that the beliefs and practices of the primitive Hebrews were hardly distinguishable from those of their heathen neighbours; in fact, we may say that they were themselves heathen. It was only as the distinctly Jewish Religion developed under the guidance of Moses and the Prophets—or, to put it the other way round, as the nature of God was gradually revealed to them—that the difference between Hebrew Religion and Heathenism became apparent. These differences became increasingly greater, until the common origin of Judaism's successor, Christianity, and heathen religion, whether modern or ancient, was for long enough unrecognized. In fact, many Christians in the past and even today consider heathen religion to be of a fundamentally different nature from Christianity—the worship not of God but of devils. Such a view has this to commend it, that it makes things so much simpler in so many ways; however, with the discoveries of modern research into the origin and development of Religion now before us, it would perhaps be foolish to deny that there is in ultimate origin and intention a real similarity between the Christian and heathen Religions, if not an actual identity, which is not merely due to imitation of Judaism and Christianity by the heathen. It needs, however, to be pointed out that the similarity has been obscured by other factors than the development of religious thought among the Jews: first, through many accretions of purely human origin in heathen religion—a tendency to combine Religion with some philosophical system; and second, by the fact that the meaning of many heathen ceremonies, in particular of sacrifice, has been changed, and a new meaning, which bears a completely different relation to the ceremony, has been substituted for the old.

Our study must therefore include not only Christianity but also heathen religions as well. In spite of the manifest differences which its various forms display in different times and in different parts of the world, Religion would appear to have a similar general underlying object—namely, the object of uniting in some mystical and symbolic fashion the worshipper and the worshipped, which also implies an existing separation between the two. This object of sacramental unity is manifestly true of what may appear to be the more refined or civilized forms of religion like Christianity and the mystery cults at the beginning of the Christian era; but it is also true of primitive religion. This is the conclusion at which Robertson Smith arrived as a result of his studies of Totemism and primitive Semitic sacrifice, even when in its later forms sacrifice seemed to have no sacramental significance. Thus, in *The Religion of the Semites* he writes:

In the course of the last lecture we were led to look with some exactness into the distinction drawn in the later ages of ancient paganism between ordinary sacrifices, where the victim is one of the animals commonly used for human food, and extraordinary or mystical sacrifices, where the significance of the rite lies in an exceptional act of communion with the godhead, by participation in holy flesh which is ordinarily forbidden to man. Analysing this distinction, and carrying back our examination of the evidence to the primitive stage of society in which sacrificial ritual first took shape, we were led to conclude that in the most ancient times all sacrificial animals had a sacrosanct character, and that no kind of beast was offered to the gods which was not too holy to be slain and eaten without a religious purpose, and without the consent and active participation of the whole clan.

For the most primitive times, therefore, the distinction drawn by later paganism between ordinary and extraordinary sacrifices disappears. In both cases the sacred function is the act of the whole community, which is conceived as a circle of brethren, united with one another and with their god by participation in one life or life-blood. The same blood is supposed to flow also in the veins of the victim, so that its death is at once a shedding of the tribal blood and a violation of the sanctity of the divine life that is transfused through every member, human or irrational, of the sacred circle. Nevertheless the slaughter of such a victim is permitted or required on solemn occasions, and all the tribesmen partake of its flesh, that they may thereby cement and seal their mystic unity with one another and with their god . . . This cement (between the worshippers and the god) is nothing else than the actual life of the sacred and kindred animal, which is conceived as residing in its flesh, but especially in its blood, and so, in the sacred meal, is actually distributed among all the participants, each of whom incorporates a particle of it with his own individual life.[1]

In brief, the primitive sacrifice is a sacramental meal through which the worshippers achieve communion with their god; and the food eaten, the life consumed, involves the death of a victim who is at once the god and the representative of the worshippers.

Even though such a theory may appear to some to be neither convincing nor acceptable on other grounds, it will be accepted as valid for the purposes of this essay, if only because it is accepted by the Psycho-analysts, and used by them in the formulation of their own theories on the origins of Religion.

This is perhaps a convenient point to emphasize the similarity both in intention and in ceremonial between the primitive pagan sacrifice and the Christian sacrament of the Holy Communion. One may, it is true, regard them both as nothing more than similar manifestations of a universal neurosis; or one may dismiss the seeming similarity as being merely accidental. But from a more sympathetic point of view the quasi-sacramental meal of the savage may be seen as a kind of type and shadow of the Christian Holy Communion; or at least as a vain groping and searching by primitive man for that unity with the object of his worship which the Christian believes to be achieved through participation in the Sacrament of the Body and Blood of Christ. The similarity

[1] *The Religion of the Semites*, pp. 312, 313.

between Christian and heathen worship has been noticed not only by modern students of Comparative Religion, but also by some of the Early Fathers, as for example, by Justin Martyr. For although he attributed the similarity to imitation of Christianity by demons, what is important is that he was aware of it, and also, so it would seem, that his heathen contemporaries were too. So, speaking of the Eucharist in his *First Apology*, he says:

> For the Apostles, in the memoirs composed by them which are called Gospels, have thus delivered unto us, what was enjoined upon them: That Jesus took bread, etc., . . . which the wicked devils have imitated in the mysteries of Mithras, commanding the same thing to be done.[1]

Again, more generally, he says, "It is not that we hold the same opinions as others, but that all speak in imitation of us."[2] In the same way even earlier the warning of Saint Paul to the Corinthians that they cannot partake in heathen and Christian worship, seems to imply that to a casual observer there can have been little apparent difference between them.[3]

If further illustration is needed, it may also be argued that this fundamental similarity in origin is shown by some of the ideas which the children of Christian parents have about God, and which are in many ways like those of heathen savages, and like them represent the ideas out of which a more highly developed religion may grow.

7. *The Psycho-analytic Theory of the Origin of Religion*

We are not for the moment directly concerned with the general Psycho-analytic theory of the origin of Totemistic Religion, as it was first put forward by Freud more than thirty years ago in his book *Totem and Taboo*, but with a

---

[1] *First Apology*, LXVI, Ante-Nicene Christian Library, p. 64.
[2] Ibid., LX, p. 58.
[3] See I Corinthians, x, 20–1: "But I say, that the things which the Gentiles sacrifice, they sacrifice to devils, and not to God: and I would not that ye should have fellowship with devils. Ye cannot drink the cup of the Lord, and the cup of devils: ye cannot be partakers of the Lord's table and of the table of devils."

particular application of that theory to a more limited sphere. In a later book, *Moses and Monotheism*, Freud put forward the argument that Hebrew Religion as it developed under the guidance of the prophets was a recollection of the religious teaching of Moses, a re-emergence from the unconscious of what the great leader and law-giver had taught, which had been repressed in the Hebrew mind because of the murder of Moses by the children of Israel in the wilderness. This monotheistic religion which Moses introduced to the Israelites was, he argues, derived from the philosophical monotheism of Ikhnaton.[1] Furthermore, this reached its climax in the religion of Paul, the teaching of Moses having returned from the unconscious in Paul as a result of the recent murder of Jesus of Nazareth, who had been thought to be Messiah, and who had himself been a kind of reincarnation of Moses. Freud begins his argument by trying to demonstrate that Moses was in fact not a Hebrew but an Egyptian. His arguments here, which are based upon Psycho-analytical, as well as historical, research, may or may not appear convincing to the student of the Old Testament. But as they do not seem to influence greatly the course of the later argument, I do not propose to discuss them in detail here. All I would say is that if Moses was brought up in the court of Pharaoh, as according to the Biblical account he was, even if not actually an Egyptian by birth, he must have appeared to his Hebrew contemporaries more as an Egyptian than as one of themselves; and anyway the religion which he taught, although in origin it may have been conditioned by his Egyptian environment, was not in itself likely to be affected by such considerations once it had been handed on. Whether he were an Egyptian or a Hebrew his own teaching remains the same: and indeed the whole of the Hebrew people who were in Egypt must have been influenced to a greater or lesser extent by their sojourn there. For the sake of argument, however, we shall accept Freud's contention that Moses was an Egyptian; but I cannot help but feel that the true psycho-

[1] Also called in English Akhenaten (I have followed the spelling used in the English translation of *Moses and Monotheism*).

logical explanation of this view is to be found not in the remote past but in Freud's own life. His general argument, which, as we shall see, depends on the belief that the early Hebrews rejected Moses and his teaching on the ground that it was imposed upon them by a foreigner, may possibly be a form of self-defence and self-justification on the part of a Jew who has himself rejected the same monotheistic religion of Moses.

Be that as it may, it is now our task to see what Freud has to say about the beginning of the Mosaic Religion and its subsequent development among the Hebrews. In order to avoid any misunderstanding or misstatement of Freud's argument, it will be best if we allow him to speak for himself, as his theory may no doubt seem rather fantastic to anyone not already familiar with Psycho-analytic reasoning. For those to whom the theory of Freud is already well-known this section may be superfluous; for those to whom it is something new it may well be inadequate. While fully aware of this difficulty, I can only hope that the former will bear it in patience and that the latter will, if this résumé is inadequate, be able to refer to Freud's own works.

Under the influence of the priests of the Sun God at On (Heliopolis), possibly strengthened by suggestions from Asia, there arose the idea of a universal God Aton—no longer restricted to one people and one country. With the young Amenhotep IV (who later changed his name to Ikhnaton) a Pharaoh succeeded to the throne who knew no higher interest than in developing the idea of such a God. He raised the Aton religion to the official religion, and thereby the universal God became the only God . . . It is the first case in the history of mankind, and perhaps the purest, of a monotheistic religion. A deeper knowledge of the historical and psychological conditions of its origin would be of inestimable value. Care was taken, however, that not much information concerning the Aton religion should come down to us. Already under the reign of Ikhnaton's weak successors everything he had created broke down . . . the Aton religion was abolished . . . Ikhnaton's reforms seemed to be but an episode, doomed to be forgotten.

This is what has been established historically, and at this

point our work of hypothesis begins. Among the intimates of Ikhnaton was a man who was perhaps called Thothmes, as so many others were at that time; the name does not matter, but its second part must have been—mose. He held high rank, and was a convinced adherent of the Aton religion, but in contra-distinction to the brooding king he was forceful and passionate. For this man the death of Ikhnaton and the abolishing of his religion meant the end of all his hopes. Only proscribed or recanting could he remain in Egypt. If he were governor of a border province he might well have come into touch with a certain Semitic tribe which had immigrated several generations ago. In his disappointment and loneliness he turned to those strangers and sought in them for a compensation of what he had lost. He chose them for his people and tried to realize his own ideals through them. After he had left Egypt with them—accompanied by his immediate followers—he hallowed them by the custom of circumcision, gave them laws, and introduced them to the Aton religion which the Egyptians had just discarded . . .

. . . Out of the darkness which the Biblical text has here left—or rather created—the historical research of our days can distinguish two facts. The first, discovered by E. Sellin, is that the Jews, who even according to the Bible were stubborn and un-ruly towards their law-giver and leader, rebelled at last, killed him and threw off the imposed Aton religion as the Egyptians had done before them. The second fact, proved by E. Meyer, is that these Jews on their return from Egypt united with tribes nearly related to them, in the country bordering on Palestine, the Sinai peninsula and Arabia, and that there in a fertile spot called Qadeš they accepted under the influence of the Arabian Midianites a new religion, the worship of the volcano god Jahve . . .

Our interest follows the fate of Moses and his doctrines, to which the revolt of the Jews only apparently put an end . . . The monotheistic idea, which had blazed up in Ikhnaton's time, was again obscured and was to remain in darkness for a long time to come.[1]

Then having pointed out the differences between the war-like Jahve and the pacific Aton, which gradually disappeared as Jahve gradually lost his own character and became more

[1] *Moses and Monotheism*, pp. 95–102.

like Moses' God, Aton, Freud goes on to set forth the significance of his hypothesis for the religion of the later Hebrews:

In three important points the later Jewish God became identical with the old Mosaic god. The first and decisive point is that he was really recognized as the only God, beside whom another god was unthinkable. Ikhnaton's monotheism was taken seriously by an entire people; indeed this people clung to it to such an extent that it became the principle content of their intellectual life and displaced all other interests. The people and the priesthood, now the dominating part of it, were unanimous on that point; but the priests, in confining their activities to elaborating the ceremonial for his worship, found themselves in opposition to strong tendencies within the people which endeavoured to revive two other doctrines of Moses about his God. The Prophets' voices untiringly proclaimed that God disdained ceremonial and sacrifice and asked nothing but a belief in Him and a life in truth and justice. When they praised the simplicity and holiness of their life in the desert they surely stood under the influence of Mosaic ideals.[1]

Having thus demonstrated that the origin of Hebrew religion lies in the doctrines which Moses had taken over from Ikhnaton, Freud proceeds to show how it was that they remained dormant for a long period, and finally prevailed among a people who had at first rejected them. He explains this dormancy and later return of Moses' teaching as a phenomenon of mass psychology, and sees a parallel in the psychology of individuals.

The only really satisfactory analogy to the remarkable process which we have recognized in the history of Jewish religion is to be found in a domain apparently remote from our problem. It is, however, very complete, approximating to identity. Here again we find the phenomenon of latency, the appearance of inexplicable manifestations which call for an explanation, and the strict condition of an early, and subsequently forgotten, experience. Here too we find the characteristic of compulsiveness, which—overpowering logical thinking—strongly engages the psychical life; it is a trait which was not concerned in the genesis of the epic.

---

[1] Ibid., p. 104.

This analogy is met with in psychopathology, in the genesis of human neurosis: that is to say, in a discipline belonging to individual psychology, whereas religious phenomena must of course be regarded as a part of mass psychology.[1]

Here we must pause in our strictly theological study to see precisely what this means. Again I shall quote at length from Freud's own work, even though it may seem only remotely connected with the subject under discussion:

> The impressions we experienced at an early age and forgot later, to which I have ascribed such importance for the ætiology of the neuroses, are called traumata. It remains an open question whether the ætiology of the neuroses should in general be regarded as a traumatic one. The objection is that a trauma is not always evident in the early history of the neurotic individual. Often we must be content to say that there is nothing else but an unusual reaction to experiences and demands that apply to all individuals; many people deal with them in another way which we may term normal . . .

> In this connection, however, two points stand out. The first is that the genesis of the neurosis always goes back to very early impressions in childhood. The second is this: it is correct to say that there are cases which we single out as "traumatic" ones because the effects unmistakably go back to one or more strong impressions of this early period. They failed to be disposed of normally, so that one feels inclined to say: if this or that had not happened, there would have been no neurosis.[2]

Freud here goes on to group together the facts which relate to the analogy between neurosis and religion. It is important that we should have them clearly in our mind, as we shall need to use them later on when we come to deal with the development of religion from a Christian point of view.

> Our researches have shown that what we call the phenomena or symptoms of a neurosis are the consequences of certain experiences and impressions which, for this very reason, we recognize to be ætiological traumata. We wish to ascertain, were it only in a rough schematic way, the characteristics common to these experiences and to neurotic symptoms.

---

[1] *Moses and Monotheism*, pp. 116, 117.   [2] Ibid., pp. 117, 118.

Let us first consider the former. All these traumata belong to early childhood, the period up to about five years . . . The experiences in question are as a rule entirely forgotten and remain inaccessible to memory. They belong to the period of infantile amnesia which is often interrupted by isolated fragmentary memories, the so-called "screen-memories".

They concern impressions of a sexual and aggressive nature and also early injuries to the self (injuries to narcissism). We should add that children at that early age do not yet distinguish between sexual and purely aggressive actions so clearly as they do later on.[1]

This theory, which it is claimed is established by analytic work,

says that, contrary to popular opinion, human sexual life—or what later corresponds with it—shows an early blossoming which comes to an end at about the age of five. Then follows the so-called latency period—lasting up to puberty—during which there is no further sexual development; on the contrary, much that has been achieved undergoes a retrogression. The theory is confirmed by anatomical study of the growth of the external genitalia . . .

The effects of the trauma are two-fold, positive and negative. The former are endeavours to revive the trauma, to remember the forgotten experience, or, better still, to make it real—to live once more through a repetition of it . . . The effects (of these "fixations on the trauma" or "repetition-compulsions") can be incorporated into the so-called normal Ego and in the form of constant tendencies lend to it immutable character traits . . . The negative reactions pursue the opposite aim; here nothing is to be remembered or repeated of the forgotten trauma . . . They express themselves in avoiding issues, a tendency which may culminate in an inhibition or phobia. These negative reactions also contribute considerably to the formation of character. Actually they represent fixations on the trauma no less than do the positive reactions, but they follow the opposite tendency. The symptoms of the neurosis proper constitute a compromise to which both the positive and negative effects of the trauma contribute . . . These opposite reactions create conflicts which the subject cannot as a rule resolve.

[1] *Moses and Monotheism*, pp. 119–20.

35

Further,

> all these phenomena, the symptoms as well as the restrictions
> of personality and the lasting changes in character, display the
> characteristic of compulsiveness; that is to say, they possess
> great physical intensity, they show a far-reaching independence
> of physical processes that are adapted to the demands of the
> real world and obey the laws of logical thinking.[1]

These observations are of very great importance in our
present study since they represent characteristics common to
both neurotic and religious phenomena. It is also significant
that the compulsive character of religious belief and of the
worship of God were well-known long before Psycho-analysis
had made the comparison with neurotic symptoms.

So far I have given, mostly in his own words, a brief
account of Freud's theory of the causation of neurosis in the
individual. It now remains for us to see how he applies this
to the subject of Religion to which it is supposed to be an
analogy. Again, even at the risk of appearing unnecessarily to
repeat what may be read elsewhere, I shall give this application largely in quotations from Freud's writings.

> Early trauma—Defence—Latency—Outbreak of the Neu-
> rosis—Partia return of the repressed material: this was the
> formula we drew up for the development of a neurosis. Now I
> will invite the reader to take a step forward and assume that in the
> history of the human species something happened similar to the
> events in the life of an individual. That is to say, mankind as a
> whole passed through conflicts of a sexual-aggressive nature,
> which left permanent traces but which were for the most part
> warded off and forgotten; later, after a long period of latency,
> they came to life again and created phenomena similar in struc-
> ture and tendency to neurotic symptoms . . . I have already
> upheld this thesis a quarter of a century ago, in my book *Totem
> and Taboo* (1912), and need only repeat what I said there.[2]

This earlier application of what is, perhaps, the most revolu-
tionary and far-reaching speculation of Psycho-analytical
research, namely, the theory of the Œdipus complex, is no
doubt well-known; but for the sake of completeness we shall

[1] *Moses and Monotheism*, pp. 121–3.   [2] Ibid., pp. 129–30.

36

repeat it here. The Œdipus complex, which takes its name from the son of Laius, king of Thebes, who killed his father and married his mother, Jocasta, was first alluded to in *The Interpretation of Dreams*, first published in 1900, and is also set out in Freud's *Introductory Lectures on Psycho-Analysis*, in which may be read the following:

> Now what does direct observation of children, at the period of object-choice before the latency period, show us in regard to the Œdipus complex? Well, it is easy to see that the little man wants his mother all to himself, finds his father in the way, becomes restive when the latter takes upon himself to caress her, and shows his satisfaction when the father goes away or is absent. . . . One might try to object that the little boy's behaviour is due to egoistic motives and does not justify the conception of an erotic complex . . . but it is soon clear that in this . . . egoistic interests only provide the occasion on which the erotic impulses seize.
>
> The first choice of object in mankind is regularly an incestuous one, directed to the mother and sister of men, and the most stringent prohibitions are required to prevent this sustained infantile tendency from being carried into effect.
>
> The clinical fact which confronts us behind the form of the Œdipus complex as established by analysis now becomes of the greatest practical importance. We learn that at the time of puberty, when the sexual instinct first asserts its demands in full strength the old familiar incestuous objects are taken up again and again invested by the libido. The infantile object-choice was but a feeble venture in play, as it were, but it laid down the direction for the object-choice of puberty. At this time a very intense flow of feeling towards the Œdipus complex or a reaction to it comes into force . . . From the time of puberty onward the human individual must devote himself to the great task of *freeing himself from the parents* . . . In neurotics, however, this detachment from the parents is not accomplished at all; the son remains all his life in subjection to his father, and incapable of transferring his libido to a new sexual object . . . in this sense the Œdipus complex is justifiably regarded as the kernel of the neuroses. [1]

I do not propose to dispute the reasonableness of this

[1] *Introductory Lectures on Psycho-Analysis*, pp. 279–83.

theory nor, at this point, to discuss the application of it which follows. We shall have occasion to say more about it at a later stage, and so for the present we shall accept it as correct, since it forms the basis of Freud's further theories, to which we must now turn our attention. In applying this hypothesis, based upon the psychology of individuals, to the psychology of the human race in its earliest times, Freud assumes a stage in the evolutionary development of man, in which

the strong male was the master and father of the whole horde: unlimited in his power, which he used brutally. All females were his property, the wives and daughters in his own horde as well as perhaps also those robbed from other hordes. The fate of the sons was a hard one; if they excited the father's jealousy they were killed or castrated or driven out. They were forced to live in small communities and to provide themselves with wives by robbing them from others . . .

The next decisive step towards changing this first kind of "social" organization lies in the following suggestion. The brothers who had been driven out and lived together in a community clubbed together, overcame the father and—according to the custom of those times—all partook of his body . . . The essential point is, however, that we attribute to those primitive people the same feelings and emotions that we elucidated in the primitives of our own times, our children, by psycho-analytic research. That is to say: they not merely hated and feared their father, but also honoured him as an example to follow; in fact each son wanted to place himself in his father's position.[1]

---

[1] *Moses and Monotheism*, pp. 130–2; see also *Totem and Taboo*, pp. 234–7.

This theory of the early organization of primitive man into hordes, each ruled by one strong and jealous male, is, as I am fully aware, not accepted by all anthropologists. Freud, however, seems to be quite emphatic on the subject, though it may seem that he justifies his views on psychological rather than anthropological grounds. One may even go so far as to say that, according to his general theory, such a stage of society, if it could not be demonstrated to have existed, would have to be assumed. When later, in Chapter III of this essay, we come to discuss the origin and significance of Totemism, I shall, in accordance with the general principle on which this essay is based, assume that such a social organization did

As a result of this killing of the father, it is suggested, the first beginnings of social law and order had their origin, for the primary purposes of establishing some sort of security, and of preventing a repetition of the crime. That this might be so, "each renounced the ideal of gaining for himself the position of father, of possessing his mother or sister," [1] in which renunciations are to be seen the origins of the two chief taboos of Totemism against murder and incest. The actual origin of Totemism is explained thus: "The memory of the father lived on during this time of the 'brother horde'. A strong animal, which perhaps at first was also dreaded, was found as a substitute." [2] This view was justified in *Totem and Taboo* [3] by the argument that the relation of the child to animals reproduces that of primitive man, and that in the analysis of boys the fear of animals is at bottom the fear of the father. The boy displaces upon an animal some of the feeling which he has for his father. This he does in order to resolve the conflict caused by his ambivalent attitude to his father, transferring his more hostile emotions to the animal, while retaining for his father his more tender emotions. In Totemism the same substitution is to be seen.

The relationship to the totem animal retained the original ambivalency of feeling towards the father. The totem was, on the one hand, the corporeal ancestor and protecting spirit of the clan; he was to be revered and protected. On the other hand, a festival was instituted on which day the same fate was meted out to him as the primeval father had encountered. He was killed and eaten by all the brothers together, [4]

which communal act of killing and eating was at once a repetition of, and an expiation for, the original crime. The conclusion of this argument is briefly as follows:

Psycho-analytic investigation of the individual teaches with

---

at one time exist; and for the justification and defence of such an assumption I must refer my readers to the works of Freud himself and of others who take a similar view of primitive society.

[1] *Moses and Monotheism*, p. 132. [2] *Ibid.*, pp. 132–3.
[3] *Totem and Taboo*, pp. 210–19. [4] *Moses and Monotheism*, p. 133.

especial emphasis that God is in every case modelled after the father and that our personal relation to God is dependent upon our relation to our physical father, fluctuating and changing with him, and that God at bottom is nothing but an exalted father.[1]

I want to state the conclusion that the beginnings of religion, ethics, society and art meet in the Œdipus complex.[2]

Having thus traced religion back to its origin, according to the Freudian theory, it is now necessary to move forward again. If, like Freud, we believe in the Scientific view of the inevitability of progress and in intellectual evolution, then it is not difficult to account for the change, which gradually took place from the theriomorphic totem to the anthropomorphic God, in terms of human intellectual development. What still remains to be seen is how from its primitive origins religion developed through Judaism to Christianity. It is claimed that as a result of Psycho-analytic research into the origin of Totemism two characteristic elements in religion may be recognized—namely, fixations on events in the remote past, and reproductions after a period of latency of what had been forgotten. Such returning memories come with great strength and force themselves with an apparently illogical and irresistible influence upon their victims, in a way precisely similar to the delusions in a psychotic case. In fact, religion is, as Freud has said, an illusion, and the universal obsessional neurosis [3] which has escaped the stigma of being branded as an abnormality because it is universal. In the case of the Religion of the Hebrews,

If we admit for the moment that the rule of Pharaoh's empire was the external reason for the appearance of the monotheistic idea, we see that this idea—uprooted from its soil and transplanted to another people—after a long latency period takes hold of this (i.e. the Hebrew) people, is treasured by them as their most precious possession and for its part keeps this people alive by bestowing on them the pride of being the chosen

---

[1] *Totem and Taboo*, p. 244. See also *New Introductory Lects., etc.,* pp. 207 ff.

[2] *Ibid.*, p. 260.   [3] *The Future of an Illusion*, pp. 24, 76.

people. It is the religion of the primeval father and the hope of reward, distinction and finally world sovereignty is bound up with it . . .

The restoration to the primeval father of his historical rights marked a great progress, but this could not be the end. The other parts of the prehistoric tragedy also clamoured for recognition. . . . It seems that a growing feeling of guiltiness had seized the Jewish people—and perhaps the whole of civilization of that time—as a precursor of the return of the repressed material. . . . Paul, a Roman Jew from Tarsus, seizes upon this feeling of guilt and correctly traced it back to its primeval source. This he called original sin; it was a crime that could be expiated only through death. Death had come into the world through original sin. In reality this crime, deserving of death, had been the murder of the Father who was later deified. The murderous deed itself, however, was not remembered; in its place stood the phantasy of expiation, and that is why this phantasy could be welcomed in the form of a gospel of salvation (Evangel). A Son of God, innocent himself, had sacrificed himself—and had thereby taken over the guilt of the world. It had to be a Son, for the sin had been the murder of the Father.

The ambivalency dominating the father-son relationship, however, shows clearly in the final result of the religious innovation. Meant to propitiate the father deity, it ends by his being dethroned and set aside. The Mosaic religion had been a Father religion; Christianity became a Son religion. The old God, the Father, took second place; Christ, the Son, stood in His stead, just as in those dark times every son had longed to do.[1]

There remains still only the question why it was that this religious development should have been unfolded among the Jews only.

The great deed and misdeed of primeval times, the murder of the Father, was brought home to the Jews, for fate decreed that they should repeat it on the person of Moses, an eminent father-substitute. . . . It can scarcely be chance that the violent death of another great man should become the starting-point for the creation of a new religion by Paul. . . . If Moses was the first Messiah, Christ became his substitute and successor . . . Then also there is some truth in the rebirth of Christ, for he

---

[1] *Moses and Monotheism*, pp. 137–41.

was the resurrected Moses and the returned primeval Father of the primitive horde as well—only transfigured and as a Son in the place of his Father.[1]

I have endeavoured to give here an account of Freud's thesis as complete as possible, and for the reasons stated earlier I have done this to a great extent by making actual quotations from his works. For a full statement and justification of his theory, however, I must refer readers to those works, and in particular to *Totem and Taboo* and *Moses and Monotheism*.

For the present I do not intend to go beyond the bounds which I laid down earlier. It is, indeed, difficult to resist the temptation to doubt much that has been put forward in the argument above, tracing the origin of Christianity back to the allegedly incestuous desires of primeval man. But to state more arguments against the different theories and speculations put forward by Freud would merely be to repeat the criticisms of Psycho-analysis already made both by Theologians and by Psychologists of other schools. Moreover, to do so now would mean abandoning the scheme of argument suggested earlier in this essay. It may later on be necessary to challenge some of the theories advocated by Freud, but for the time being we shall in general accept his theories where they are plainly dependent upon purely Psycho-analytic or historical research and not on merely imaginative conjecture; and we shall also allow the validity of the analogy between neurotic obsessions and religious observances.

There appears, however, to be one point in his argument where Freud does not really seem satisfied: that is in the question of the immediate origin of Ikhnaton's monotheism; and it is from this point that I propose to start. Freud himself seems to be aware of this weakness, when he says, "A deeper

[1] Ibid., pp. 143–5. It is, however, significant that in the mind of Paul it was not so much Moses as Adam who was the type of Christ; see 1 Corinthians, xv, 45, 47: "And so it is written, The first man Adam was made a living soul; the last Adam was made a quickening spirit . . . The first man is of the earth, earthy: the second man is the Lord from heaven."

knowledge of the historical and psychological conditions of its origin would be of inestimable value. Care was taken, however, that not much information concerning the Aton religion should come down to us."[1] Later on, however, he makes a more positive suggestion: "In Egypt monotheism had grown—so far as we understand its growth—as an ancillary effect of imperialism; God was the reflection of a Pharaoh autocratically governing a great world empire."[2] This can hardly be considered as a valid explanation of the sudden beginning of what was to all intents and purposes apparently a new religion with no roots in the past, particularly when we consider that the pacific God Aton was very different in character from the general type of an imperialist Pharaoh—unless, indeed, his character was moulded on that of Ikhnaton himself. Nor is it a sufficient reason for a man, with a character far different from that of Ikhnaton, such as Moses is represented as having, to continue the religion of a collapsed empire. If Ikhnaton's monotheistic religion was "an ancillary effect of imperialism", it was hardly likely to persist after the fall of the Empire which had given it its birth. If we would find the cause of Moses' monotheism we must, therefore, look deeper.

A second question, arising from the historical background upon which Freud has built his theory, is how far it is correct to assume a direct influence by Ikhnaton upon Moses. In *Moses and Monotheism* the date of Moses is assumed to be in the latter part of the fourteenth century before Christ, within a comparatively short time of the death of Ikhnaton, which is placed before 1350 B.C. It is, however, not an easy matter to date the Exodus exactly, and so I do not intend to discuss this rather vexed question in detail, as I am not competent to do so. I would, therefore, only point out that the date of the Exodus which Freud favours—and, we may add, which favours Freud—is only one of those which have been suggested by Old Testament scholars. Three possible dates are given by T. H. Robinson[3]—namely, (a) between 1600 and

[1] *Moses and Monotheism*, p. 96.   [2] Ibid., p. 105.
[3] Oesterly and Robinson, *History of Israel*, Vol. I, pp. 71 ff.

43

1480, (b) between 1380 and 1300, and (c) after 1200. If, therefore, Moses was not a contemporary of Ikhnaton some other explanation must be given of the origin of the monotheistic religion which Moses taught.

Considering these two points together—namely, the uncertainty as to the origin of Ikhnaton's monotheism, and the possible doubt as to the exact date of Moses—and remembering also that, according to the Psycho-analytic theory we have examined above, the monotheism of the Prophets and of Paul was a return of repressed material, we may hazard the guess that monotheism in either Ikhnaton or Moses or in both was a similar return of repressed material: that is to say, in other words, that monotheistic religion had existed at some time before either Ikhnaton or Moses, and had been repressed by generations long before their time. If this is so, then it means that pure monotheistic belief may, in a repressed and therefore unconscious form, have existed among our remotest ancestors, in a way similar to that in which it existed in a repressed and unconscious form among the Hebrews after the death of Moses.

8. *The Conscious and the Unconscious: Repression*

To justify this conjecture on grounds which may be acceptable to the Psycho-analyst we must be certain that we follow exactly Psycho-analytic theory: and also, that this justification may be followed by those who are not familiar with the general principles of Psycho-analysis, some account must now be given of the relationship between conscious and unconscious mental processes, and also of that mode of reaction to psychical difficulties which is called Repression.

As is no doubt well-known, and as has been pointed out earlier in this essay, the Freudian system of Psychology began as a method of medical treatment for those who suffered from nervous disorders. In the course of this purely clinical work it was discovered that the dreams of patients undergoing treatment could be interpreted by the physician in such a way that facts about the true mental state of the patient came to light that other methods of treatment, such as hypnosis, had failed to discover.

> One day the discovery was made that the symptoms of disease in certain nervous patients have meaning. It was upon this discovery that the psycho-analytic method of treatment was based. In this treatment it happened that patients in speaking of their symptoms also mentioned their dreams, whereupon the suspicion arose that these dreams too had meaning . . .
>
> Our aim is to demonstrate the meaning of dreams, in preparation for the study of the neurosis. There are good grounds for this reversal of procedure, since the study of dreams is not merely the best preparation for that of the neurosis, but a dream is itself a neurotic symptom and, moreover, one which possesses for us the incalculable advantage of occurring in healthy people.[1]

To understand fully, therefore, the Freudian theory of the mind and its processes—a theory which embraces both the normal and the abnormal—it would be necessary to give a fairly full account of the Psycho-analytic theory of dreams. As this, however, would lead us too far from the course of our enquiry, I do not intend to go into it here, but only to give the conclusions which are relevant to this study.[2] Freud divides the mind into three parts or systems—the conscious, the preconscious and the unconscious. As the child grows up he receives impressions from the world around him by means of his various senses, particularly by sight and hearing. It is these impressions which form the preconscious aspect of the mind, and they are readily accessible to the individual, who can remember or recall such impressions at will or, in other words, bring them into his conscious system. Naturally, as experience increases, so too the content of the preconscious system increases, but it will nevertheless remain constantly

[1] Freud: *Introductory Lects., etc.*, p. 67.

[2] For a full statement of Freud's theory of dreams I must refer the reader to *The Interpretation of Dreams*, and to Part II of his *Introductory Lects., etc.*, together with the first chapter of his *New Introductory Lects., etc.* (Lecture XXIX). A clear and concise account of it is also given in *An Introduction to Abnormal Psychology* by V. E. Fisher, pp. 416–24. See also William Brown: *Psychology and Psychotherapy* (Chapters IV and V).

available, and our conscious thought constantly draws upon this supply. But such reception of impressions by the sensory perceptions is not the only activity of the child. As has been mentioned earlier, the sexual instincts and energies of the child seek for expression, and find it in the form of an attachment to some object in his environment, usually, when the child is a boy, to his mother. This infantile sexual object-choice, in the form of an attachment to the parent of the opposite sex is known as the Œdipus complex. As the child grows older, however, a tension or conflict arises between two sets of feelings within him—between his sexual feelings for his mother, on the one hand, and, on the other, his developing sense of personality, including within it the sense of propriety and morals. This conflict generally resolves itself by means of a repression, that is a forcing into the unconscious system of the erotic feelings towards the mother, which thus becomes a model for the repression of subsequent unwelcome thoughts and concepts, or of desires and wishes which are incompatible with the moral consciousness. Thus the unconscious system is, as it were, at first inhabited by the repressed Œdipus complex, but is later filled by other repressed material and so, like the preconscious system, continues to expand. The great difference, however, between the unconscious and the preconscious systems, is that whereas the thoughts and concepts—the impressions—contained by the preconscious can come into, and go out of, consciousness without let or hindrance, the same is not true of the unconscious. The content of the unconscious system is kept repressed, or, as we may say, imprisoned, by a kind of mental mechanism which Freud at first called the Censor or the Psychic Censorship, but in his later writings the Ego-Ideal, or Super-Ego, so that thoughts, desires and wishes, contained in the unconscious cannot be called forth into consciousness at will, as can the content of the preconscious. It is claimed, however, that in such states as that of the dream, the censorship, which appears to be part of the preconscious system, relaxes its vigilance and repressed desires and wishes unwelcome in a waking state are able to slip out of the unconscious during sleep and manifest themselves as dreams. They cannot do this, however, openly, but have still to elude the censorship by means of a system of symbolization and distortion, as a result of which the censorship is in a sense cheated, and the consciousness of the sleeper left undisturbed as it does not recognize the real significance of the symbols. There are thus two aspects of the dream ; first the manifest dream content, which is what the sleeper actually experiences; and secondly, the latent dream-content, the real meaning of the dream, which it is claimed can only be discovered through the analysis of its manifest content. This distinction is of great importance, and we shall have occasion to refer to it again later on.

. This description of the Psycho-analytic theory of the dream may appear to be somewhat of a digression, but it is of use because it helps to make clear the nature of repression and the work of the Psychic censorship. Freud himself clarifies the difference between the unconscious, preconscious and conscious systems in this way:

> The crudest conception of these systems is the one we shall find most convenient, a spatial one. The unconscious system may therefore be compared to a large ante-room, in which the various mental excitations are crowding upon one another, like individual beings. Adjoining this is a second, smaller apartment, a sort of reception-room, in which consciousness resides. But on the threshold between the two there stands a personage with the office of door-keeper, who examines the various mental excitations, censors them, and denies them admittance to the reception-room when he disapproves of them ... Now this metaphor may be employed to widen our terminology.

When the mental excitations

> have pressed forward to the threshold and been turned back by the door-keeper, they are *"incapable of becoming conscious"*; we call them *repressed*. But even those excitations which are allowed over the threshold do not necessarily become conscious ... This second chamber therefore may be suitably called *the pre-conscious system*.[1]

---

[1] *Introductory Lects., etc.,* p. 249.

In spite of the crudeness of this spatial metaphor, and its unscientific nature, it is, Freud asserts, "an extensive approximation to actual reality". In Freud's later thought the censorship between the unconscious and preconscious systems was identified as a function of the Ego-Ideal or Super-Ego. Of this Freud says:

> In the course of individual development a part of the inhibiting forces in the outer world become internalized; a standard is created in the Ego, which opposes the other faculties by observation, criticism and prohibition. We call this new standard the *super-ego* . . . The super-ego is the successor and representative of the parents (and educators), who superintended the actions of the individual in his first years of life; it perpetuates their functions almost without a change.[1]

If we now compare what has been said immediately above concerning the content of the unconscious system with what has been said earlier about the latency of the monotheistic idea among the Hebrews after Moses, we shall be led to this conclusion: that the content of the unconscious system can be distinguished as belonging to two classes, first the desires and wishes of the infant as an individual which have been repressed during his own life, and secondly an inherited store of repressed concepts and desires which have been passed on to the child from the past. Such a tradition or transmission of repressed material must be assumed to have taken place through individual minds, which together make up the mass, if a theory is to be put forward for the transmission of monotheism from the time of Moses down to Paul, when we take into account the long period of its latency which Freud supposes. Indeed in putting forward this theory of unconscious transmission Freud naturally accepts this view, though he says that in this analogy "repressed" is not used in its technical sense.[2] It seems rather to be a case of the material remaining in a state of repression than of it being actually repressed by each individual.[3]

[1] *Moses and Monotheism*, pp. 183–4.
[2] *Moses and Monotheism*, p. 208.
[3] See *Totem and Taboo*, p. 262.

48

While remaining fully aware of the later differences in theory between Freud and C. G. Jung, it may at this point be of interest to compare this distinction of the content of the unconscious into two classes with Jung's distinction into the personal unconscious and the collective unconscious, which he defines as follows:

> The personal unconscious consists of all those contents that have become unconscious, either because, their intensity being lost, they were forgotten, or because consciousness has withdrawn from them, i.e. so-called repression. Finally, this layer contains those elements—partly sense perceptions—which on account of too little intensity have never reached consciousness, and yet in some way have gained access into the psyche. The collective unconscious, being an inheritance of the possibilities of ideas, is not individual, but generally human, generally animal even, and represents the real foundations of the individual soul.[1]

In spite of its apparent similarity, such a system is manifestly different from that of Freud, who rejects the idea—and the necessity of the idea—of the collective unconscious. "I do not think that much is to be gained by introducing the concept of a 'collective' unconscious—the content [of the unconscious is collective anyhow, a general possession of mankind."[2]

9. *Reconstruction of the Freudian Analogy*

It is now our task to consider once again the origin of the Christian religion in the light of Psycho-analytic investigations. This time, however, the examination will be carried out from the religious point of view: in other words we shall start with the presupposition that God exists, while at the same time making use of that part of Psycho-analytic theory which is based upon the actual treatment and observation of neurotic patients, and which therefore the Theologian is not in a position to dispute. I mean by this the discoveries relating to the formation of neurosis, and following from that

[1] *Contributions to Analytical Psychology*, p. 110.
[2] *Moses and Monotheism*, p. 208.

the general theories on the nature of the human mind—the conscious and the unconscious—and the phenomenon of repression.

The Freudian reconstruction of the history of religion depends on the analogy with the ætiology and development of a neurosis. In this reconstruction a similar course will be pursued. It will therefore be well if we bear in mind the formula which Freud drew up for the development of a neurosis: Early Trauma—Defence—Latency—Outbreak of the Neurosis—Partial return of the Repressed material. We shall assume that this analogy is valid, and that the account given by Freud of the development of Hebrew Religion after Moses is a correct application of this analogy, as far, that is, as it concerns the latency of the monotheistic idea in the time immediately after Moses. We cannot, however, agree with Freud's view of the history of Jesus Christ as it is recorded in the Gospels, and we can disagree not on psychological but on critical and historical grounds. Freud's view seems to affirm, on the basis of a purely rationalistic interpretation, which unfortunately is also to be found in the writings of some who profess to be Christian, that the Jesus of history is no more than a myth: or, more explicitly, that although there may have been a man called Jesus of Nazareth whom a certain number of individuals believed to be the Messiah, the Christian Religion is in fact no more than an invention of Paul. With such a view the Christian finds himself in direct disagreement, on historical and critical grounds. I do not intend to argue here for the general historical truth of the accounts of Jesus' life and teaching in the gospels; I would only point out that Freud must possess a curiously selective critical faculty, when it comes to dealing with historical personages, which appears to accept facts which favour his theories and to reject facts which do not. However, it is, I think, sufficiently plain from the history of the primitive Church, that although the influence of Paul on the development and interpretation of Christian theology is not to be denied nor underestimated, yet the Christian Religion would still have existed without him. Were we to exclude from the

New Testament the whole influence, direct or indirect, of Paul, there would still remain a clear and complete basis for the Christian Faith. We cannot, therefore, accept the implication of the Freudian view that Christianity rests simply on the teaching of Paul, nor that "in reality we have hardly more definite knowledge of him (Jesus) than we have of Moses". Nor can we agree that "we do not know if he really was the great man whom the gospels depict, or whether it was not rather the fact and the circumstances of his death that were the decisive factor in his achieving importance".[1] It appears, I believe, to be idle to attempt to deny the historicity of the written records of the life of Jesus, unless we are prepared also to deny the historicity of the accounts of the lives of other people in the past when it does not suit our purpose to believe them.

If we are to deny the Freudian view of the immediate origin of Christianity as it is set out in *Moses and Monotheism*, we may wonder if any other view can be put forward which will account for its emergence: that is, of course, a view which will be in harmony with the general Psycho-analytic theory of the return of repressed material after a period of latency. It is here then that I intend to put forward a suggestion as to the origin of Christianity, which, given the presupposition that there is an eternal God—more, that is, than merely the deified human father—appears to be as plausible as the suggestion put forward by Freud. Stated in a few words, it is this: that the special doctrines of the Christian Faith came into the conscious mind of Jesus Christ from his own unconscious system. It other words, Christianity is a return of repressed material: the teaching of Jesus, which alone makes his death of significance to the Christian, is, I would suggest, a recollection from the unconscious system of humanity present in Jesus: a recollection of a concept previously held in the conscious mind of our remotest ancestor, but subsequently repressed in the unconscious. If this is so, then there must have been some trauma—some experience in the infancy of the human race—which caused

[1] *Moses and Monotheism*, p. 144.

this material to be repressed. This, indeed, may sound nothing new, nor anything which really contradicts what Freud has said, except in the matter of the person through whom the repressed material returned from repression. The difference, however, lies not in the *mode* of the repression or of the return of the repressed material, but rather in the actual nature of the material repressed—the *content* of the unconscious.

The Christian Faith, presupposing the existence of God, affirms that the original cause of human misery is the loss of communion with God, which is itself a result of human sin. As we have already seen, it is the aim of all religion to re-establish this lost communion, the chief result of which, in the history of the world, has been a legacy of sinfulness handed on from one generation to another. The Psycho-analyst, however, viewing life from a purely anthropocentric standpoint, holds that the abnormalities of human conduct are caused through a lack of balance—a conflict or tension—in the conscious mind, because the desires of the Ego come into conflict with the directing force of the Super-Ego. This conflict is resolved by the repression of the unwelcome desires, of which the repression of the Œdipus complex is the type and pattern. These repressed desires, however, continue to exert themselves even in a state of repression, and it is to this that we must attribute what is usually known as moral evil: and, moreover, as we have seen, the repressed desires and thoughts of one generation may be transmitted to subsequent ones. Now, if we allow for the difference of the terminology employed, we shall see that a similarity, so great that it amounts almost to an identity, exists between the Christian doctrines of Original Sin, as the cause of evil in the world, and the Psycho-analytic theory of inherited tendencies transmitted in a repressed form through the unconscious. This similarity, however, must not blind us to the difference of thought with respect to moral values revealed in the two theories, a difference which springs from the difference of the presuppositions underlying them.

As we have had occasion to point out earlier, Freud has

suggested that the origin of evil (i.e. moral evil), and therefore the origin of morality and religion, is due to the first murder of the father by the sons in order to gain possession of the mother. They committed this sexual-aggressive crime because of the allegedly natural incestuous desire of sons towards their mothers—the Œdipus complex.[1] Because of this murder, subsequent generations repress the incestuous desire and the sense of guilt which resulted from the crime. There seems, however, to be a weakness in this argument. It hardly seems sufficient to adduce social security as the cause of something with such far-reaching consequences as the communal sense of guilt felt by the primeval parricides. We are legitimately entitled to ask this question: why should the sons feel a sense of remorse and guilt for this crime, unless it was, like the sin of Adam, the transgression of a prohibition already implanted in the mind; that is, an act in defiance of what the Christian would call "conscience".[2] The sense of guilt arising from this primeval crime seems to force us back to belief in some underlying natural law. Morality must, as Saint Paul has pointed out,[3] come before sin: or, to put it more exactly, morality must come before the full awareness of the real character of the act, whether that act is evil or good. We must not forget that it is possible to perform an act which is in fact evil, without at the time knowing its true character, and for it to be realized as a sin and so to result in a feeling of guilt only after its performance and after the realization of its evil nature. But if its nature is thus realized after the event, we must suppose some latent moral consciousness existing before the commission of the act. This latent moral awareness is really analogous to what is called the conscience, for the conscience, which may be defined as

[1] See *Totem and Taboo*, p. 260.
[2] A simple answer to this question of the origin of the sense of guilt would be to say that in killing the father the sons were in fact transgressing the father's command: this, however, does not fit in with Psycho-analytic theory, as it places law, and therefore also morality, *before* and not *after* the murder of the father.
[3] Romans, vii, 7: "I had not known sin, but by the law: for I had not known lust, except the law had said, Thou shalt not covet."

"the voice of the repressed good",[1] normally seems to function only in persons who have already committed sin. In other words, we are brought back to the idea of an absolute moral law in man, and yet independent of man, existing from the beginning, though it may justifiably be suggested that this moral law was not consciously realized until after man had sinned. Moreover, it is this absolute moral law which is the force which ultimately moulds the Super-Ego, while parents and educators are themselves temporal vehicles of this absolute law.

The first sin of man was thus an act against an absolute moral standard, and not merely the expression of a social revolution. Remembering, therefore, that we are presupposing the existence of God as the foundation on which this reconstruction is built, we would define the first sin of man —the trauma at the root of the universal neurosis—as an act committed not against man but against God.[2] The first man, created in the image and likeness of God, was at first without sin, and therefore, like a new-born babe, unrepressed, naked and unashamed, and lived in perfect communion with God.[3] Human sin broke this communion, and as a result man ceased to know God face to face. The question as to what was the precise nature of this sin we shall leave aside for the present; all we shall say here is that it was, as it were by definition, a sin against God—an act in transgression of the absolute moral law. The multiplication of sins—a cumulative effect of the first break with God—caused an increase, or a deepening, in

[1] Hadfield: *Psychology and Morals*, p. 44.

[2] For a full statement of the nature of this act, see Chapter II.

[3] It is, I hope, hardly necessary for me to justify my use of the term "the first man". This is not a fundamentalist view of the origin of man. All I mean by "the first man" or by "Adam" is the first creature that had ceased to be animal and was identifiable as human —a stage which we are entitled to assume if we take the evolutionary development of the embryo and then the infant as a pattern of the development of the human race. Moreover, I believe that it is necessary, if we believe in the moral reality of human sin—that it is not just part of an evolutionary process—to assume that the first man had a conscious access to, and knowledge of, God, which is what we mean by living in communion with God.

the ignorance of God and a widening of the breach between the creature and the Creator. The human mind now felt God to be a kind of external force who had no right to meddle with the affairs of man; and so man was consequently more and more unwilling to submit himself to the will of God, which he still perceived as the moral law through the conscience, because such submission was at variance with fallen humanity's desire to call one's soul one's own and not God's to whom in fact it still belonged. But the sense of guilt, resulting from sin, could not be completely obliterated and forgotten; it remained constantly repressed in the unconscious—the awareness of sin in the similitude of Adam's sin, ἐφ' ᾧ πάντες ἥμαρτον,[1] and with it also the knowledge of God once possessed in the conscious mind of Adam, but repressed now because it was repugnant to the new self-sufficient and self-assertive spirit of man.[2] This repressed knowledge of God, however, after the pattern of the repressed material of the individual, returned from the unconscious from time to time partially and imperfectly, as such repressed material may do in a dream distorted and incomplete. It is, I would suggest, to this partial return of repressed material that the origin of Totemism, its beliefs and its ceremonies, are to be attributed; and, moreover, it may well have been such recollections from the unconscious as these, what Freud calls "screen-memories", that gave rise to the belief in a Golden Age in the remote past, when men and gods could live and move together. Thus it came about that man, aware of an unconscious disharmony within him caused through sin, endeavoured in his conscious mind to regain through religion some unknown entity, which was in fact that communion with, and knowledge of, God which his soul desired, but which were repressed and, as it were, locked up in his

[1] Romans, v, 12: see also Beyschlag: *New Testament Theology*, Vol. II, pp. 59–60; Sanday and Headlam: Romans, pp. 133–4.

[2] Compare Romans, i, 28: . . . καθὼς οὐκ ἐδοκίμασαν τὸν Θεὸν ἔχειν ἐν ἐπιγνώσει. In this respect, also, we should notice that it is belief in God and not belief in science which undermines man's own opinions of himself: it is Science rather than Religion which thus appears to be the wish-fulfilment.

unconscious. It was, we may suggest, from this conscious striving, reinforced by what were in fact imperfect and distorted glimpses of the truth hidden in the unconscious, that "religion" took its origin, and under their influence gradually developed. Perfect knowledge of God, however, could not be reached because of the imperfection of the recollection—or, in other words, because the repressive force of the censorship, or the resistance of the Super-Ego, was too great to allow a complete and undistorted return of the repressed material. It was only when a man was born without the blight of original sin (or, without the inherited repressions of his earthly ancestors), but with a complete human personality (including as an integral part of itself the inherited content of the unconscious now released from repression and so capable of being brought back into the conscious system), that mankind could regain through him the lost communion with God. This man, Jesus Christ, was thus truly the second Adam; but he was perfect where Adam had been imperfect, in as much as all human experience was gathered up in him, and humanity's repressions overcome in him by God's new creation.[1] If this hypothesis is correct, then it would appear that the religion of Jesus, the essential feature of which was salvation, or the re-establishing of a lost communion with God, was held in the unconscious mind of man by repression, and could only be released by a person who could fulfil the requirements of a true analyst of the soul.

Nothing has here been said about the work of Saint Paul, to whom Freud attributes the real founding of the Christian Religion. If we accept the Christian belief in the general trustworthiness of the Gospel narratives, then, as has been pointed out earlier, we cannot agree with his assertion. Saint Paul, however, remains a most important figure in the growth of Christianity, as an interpreter of the faith taught by Jesus. Thus, to a limited extent, Freud may be correct: the recent death of Jesus, or possibly the death of Stephen at which Paul was himself present, may have acted as a sufficient

[1] For a full development of this idea, and a statement of its significance, see Chapter III.

56

stimulus to cause a certain return of repressed material which enabled him to see the teaching and the death of Jesus in their true light. Paul himself affirms that he had received his Gospel not from man but from God,[1] by which we are to understand not the facts of Christ's life and teaching, but the interpretation of those facts.

Apart from any objections to the general treatment of this subject from the point of view of Psycho-analysis there are two other points to which orthodox Christians may take exception: namely, the views put forward concerning the nature of what we call Divine Revelation, and of heathen religion. These two objections really depend upon one another; they are in fact two forms of the same objection. About the latter, the nature of heathen religion, I hope it has been shown that such a view is not incompatible with the belief that Christianity is unique, and is to be regarded as the final form of religion, so far, that is, as anything in this world may be regarded as final. I believe that heathen religions, however primitive and barbaric, are to be regarded as the outward manifestations of the searching of the human mind for that truth about God which is locked in the unconscious and only released in its completeness by Christ; Christianity is thus the fulfilment of the religious strivings of the world. Such a view seems to be in accordance with the words of Saint Paul to the Athenians in Acts, xvii, 23.[2] It is also shown by the fact of conversion to Christianity; in it the convert recognizes the thing for which he has been looking.[3] This, of course, does not mean that heathen religions are to be regarded in any

---

[1] Galatians, i, 11 f.: "But I certify you, brethren, that the gospel which was preached of me is not after man. For I neither received it of man, neither was I taught it, but by the revelation of Jesus Christ."

[2] "For as I passed by, and beheld your devotions, I found an altar with this inscription, TO THE UNKNOWN GOD. Whom therefore ye ignorantly worship, him declare I unto you." At any rate, even if these words are not actually Pauline, they no doubt express the thought of the author of Acts and of many early Christians with him.

[3] Compare St. Augustine, *Confessions*, I, 1: "Thou madest us for Thyself, and our heart is restless until it repose in Thee."

sense as of equal value or efficacy with Christianity. They may be signs of the groupings and strivings of the human mind, but, we must remember, of a mind diseased by sin. Any naïve idea that they are true parallels or equivalents of Christianity must be cast aside, in spite of their apparent identity of purpose and common origin. When later on we come to examine more fully the nature of Christian belief we shall be able to correct, I hope, such inaccurate views; for the present, however, it must suffice to give this warning and refer readers to the latter part of the third chapter of this essay. Of the nature of revelation, also, we shall have occasion to speak again, and until that time I propose to reserve my defence.

10. *Conclusion*

The reconstruction of the origin and development of religion, which I have tried to give here, was based on the presupposition of belief in God, and as it has gradually unfolded itself the reasonableness of religion, according to such a view of it, has I hope been demonstrated. When, however, a parallel reconstruction was made, with the implicit presupposition of belief in the non-existence of God, religion seemed wholly unreasonable—unless belief in God were to have been thrown in at the end, like a sort of *deus ex machina*, to restore the situation. In other words, with the presupposition that there is a God, who has created man in his own image, the reasonableness of religion in general and of Christianity in particular may be demonstrated as logically and as forcibly as, from the opposite presupposition that God does not exist, it may be argued that God has been created in the human mind in the image of the deified father of the primeval horde. Indeed in our sense this latter proposition is true, but not in the sense that Freud meant. From a religious point of view the primitive father is a "type" of God.[1] Such

---

[1] Compare Ephesians, iii, 14–15: "For this cause I bow my knees unto the Father of our Lord Jesus Christ, of whom all fatherhood in heaven and earth is named."

an idea of the human family and the human father, upon which the stability of society rests, may be a recollection of the true psychological relationship of man to God, as well as of the child to his earthly father. Indeed, the authority of the parent is no more than an extension of the authority of God. In the same way the so-called Super-Ego may be regarded not so much as an internalization of the influence of parents and educators, though indeed it is partly this, as the latent sense of absolute morality—the influence of the moral creator.

In the Psycho-analytic examination of the materials provided by the critical and comparative studies of religion it is not, I would suggest, the scientific method which proves the psycho-analytic theory against religious belief, except in so far as that method depends upon the anthropocentric view of life. Rather, I would contend, it is the presupposition underlying the Psycho-analytic theory that is the real foundation of its argument and that conditions its conclusion. The method itself neither proves nor disproves the truths of the Christian Religion.

Indeed, the Psycho-analytic method may prove to be a two-edged weapon which may be turned effectively upon its creator. In criticizing what he calls the religious *Weltanschauung*, Freud gives what he believes to be the causes of the strength of religion, and concludes that the infant's needs for information about the world, for security in the world, and for precepts to guide him in his life, all of which are satisfied by his parents, are carried over by the grown man into his religion, of which these infantile desires form the real foundation. Further, he regards religion as a necessary step—but still only a step—in the cultural development of man, or as the universal neurosis which will in time be cured. If in such ways, by Psycho-analysis, Freud can find reasons for man's purely irrational and unwarrantable belief in God, the religious man too may be able by similar methods to find equally plausible reasons for Freud's vehement denial of God. It is not my purpose to Psycho-analyse Freud or to give Psycho-analytic reasons for the phenomenon of atheism; I would only point out that Freud was a lapsed Jew and an atheist *before* he invented Psycho-analysis, and that his hostility to religion may be found to have an endopsychic explanation, as an attempt to justify his own lack of belief. The onus of proof rests as much upon the atheist to disprove the existence of God, as it does upon the believer to prove it. Moreover, if it is argued against religion that belief in God arises from a wish-fulfilment on the part of the believer, it may also be suggested, by a corresponding argument, that disbelief in God arises from an unconscious desire that God should not exist.

My purpose, however, will have been achieved if what is written above merely exposes the unreasonableness of the arguments brought against religion by the anti-religious psychology of Freud, and so transfers the controversy to its proper sphere, which is the study of absolute presuppositions.

THE SENSE OF SHAME AND THE
ORIGIN OF SIN

1. *Introduction*

IN the last chapter we had occasion to mention the sin of Adam as being the "trauma" which was at the root of man's repression of the knowledge of God. As has already been pointed out, Freud sees the origin of religion in a crime against man; while on the other hand I have put forward the suggestion from a Christian point of view that the first crime of humanity, the sin of Adam, was a sin against God.

In Christian theological teaching about the origin of sin, the primary sin of Adam has been explained as pride by some schools of thought and as concupiscence by others; while by some authors, and in particular one may mention Saint Augustine, the origin of sin is given sometimes as the one, sometimes as the other—as pride in the race, and concupiscence in the individual. It would, however, appear reasonable to suppose that if either pride or concupiscence was the first sin or the cause of sin, then certainly they could not both be, unless some essential connection can be established between these two things which at first sight appear to be mutually exclusive. It is the primary object of this chapter to show that a connection of this kind does in fact exist, though in reaching this conclusion the argument may appear to take rather a long time, and to follow an unduly circuitous route, travelling into realms not normally frequented by the Theologian. But in defence of this, I can only say that I am presenting the course of the argument in the same way by which I myself reached the conclusion, and which therefore appears to me the most logical form in which to set it out. Although the conclusion may in a sense appear self-evident once it has been reached, it appears to me to be worth while to cover all the various steps by which it was reached, since in the process we move out of the realm of what is strictly Theology into that of Psychology; and, although to some this consideration may appear totally irrelevant, to others it may perhaps show how a closer study of human thought-processes may help us to elucidate theological problems. In our present state, bounded as we are by our earthly limitations, we can only know of Divine-Human relations from the human point of view, and can only describe God, whom we see at best as it were "through a glass darkly", by analogy. If therefore we would hope to know more about our Religion, we must base that knowledge not upon speculation about the nature of God, but upon a closer study of the nature of man—on the half of the Divine-Human axis which we are in a position to study. In other words, we can only know the Creator as he is reflected in his creatures, and so they must form the subject of our study. It will, therefore, be a secondary purpose of this chapter and the next to show how Psychology, the study of the human mind, may help to throw some light on a Theological problem.

2. *The Sense of Shame and Nakedness*

The first apparent result of the fall from original innocence on the part of our first parents, Adam and Eve, was the awareness that they were naked; and this in its turn produced a sense of shame which they had not experienced before. "And they were both naked, the man and his wife, and were not ashamed . . . And the eyes of them both were opened, and they knew that they were naked; and they sewed fig leaves together, and made themselves aprons." [1] Before their sin they had been, as are the beasts, naked and yet not ashamed; but afterwards they hid themselves from God, who, we read, first knew of their sin from the confession made by Adam that he was ashamed of his nakedness. "And the Lord God called unto the man, and said unto him, Where art thou? And he said, I heard Thy voice in the garden, and I was afraid, because I was naked, and I hid myself. And he said,

[1] Genesis, ii, 25, and iii, 7.

Who told thee that thou wast naked? Hast thou eaten of the tree whereof I commanded thee that thou shouldest not eat?"[1]

Adam after the Fall and almost all subsequent generations of humanity share in this peculiar sense of shame at being found naked or only partially clothed. This statement may appear to be rather a sweeping generalization, and it may be argued that this sense of shame is not shared by all people throughout the world, but is felt only by certain races. The notable exceptions are: certain savage tribes who are habitually naked, or who have assumed clothing only after they have been in contact with some external civilization: the classical Greeks: certain sects, such as the Adamites, who cultivated nudity for religious or ethical reasons: and the modern so-called "Naturists". These four classes may, however, be divided into two distinct categories—those who have never worn clothes, and those who have intentionally discarded clothing as a matter of principle. Of the former it should be noted that they are of a generally low standard of civilization (in its broadest sense), and have not reached a standard of moral discrimination comparable with that, for example, of the primitive Hebrews among whom the Genesis story of man's fall originated. Moreover, we must take into account the fact that man's first sin and his consequent realization of it was a slow process, like the process of his creation. If this is so, then the naked savages to today may be regarded as being outside the scope of this study, since they are a relic of man's history before the dawn of complete moral consciousness.

This, at any rate, appears to be true of certain tribes of the Sakai and the Semang in the Malay Peninsula, who seem to be completely unaware of their nakedness, and who also display what may be called a pre-moral outlook on behaviour in general, like that of the very young child.[2]

[1] Genesis, iii, 9–11.
[2] For this information, and for that about prisoners of war in Japanese hands, I am indebted to my cousin, Mr. P. J. Gibbs Pancheri, who was in Malaya before and during the Japanese occupation.

With the classical Greeks, however, this is not the case since, normally they wore clothing and only stripped for particular purposes such as athletic sports. Here nudity was practised consciously and intentionally, and was not the natural unashamed nakedness of the savage: if it was unashamed, use had made it so. In Homeric times nakedness was regarded as something of which men were naturally ashamed, as may be gathered from the account of Odysseus' encounter with Nausicaa,[1] but the "nudism" of Classical Greece, if it is legitimate to compare it with the acceptance of paederasty as a normal form of sexual love, appears thus to be an unnatural form of behaviour, which easily led to the calculated depravity of Hellenistic and Roman times. The same may also be said of the so-called "Naturist" cults of the present day. If it is true that the modern nudist is really "naked and unashamed", then we must be prepared to consider whether or not this is so because in modern society the moral standards of many have fallen: that if they are unashamed, it is rather because shame has been lost, than because it has never been known or has been overcome by a real conquest of sin, though this must not be taken as a wholesale imputation of immorality to

[1] See *Odyssey*, VI, 127 ff.

> ὣς εἰπὼν θάμνων ὑπεδύσετο δῖος Ὀδυσσεύς,
> ἐκ πυκινῆς δ᾿ ὕλης πτόρθον κλάσε χειρὶ παχείῃ
> φύλλων, ὡς ῥύσαιτο περὶ χροῒ μήδεα φωτός.

In the very primitive story the branch was plucked up by Odysseus, not so much to cover his nakedness, as to be a token of supplication, as such branches were used in classical times (compare Sophocles: Œdipus Tyrannus, 1–3, 19–21). The similarity in language and thought between Homer's description of Odysseus' encounter with Nausicaa and the Biblical account of Adam and Eve sewing together fig-leaves (Genesis, iii, 7) may lead us to suppose that our first parents did this also as a token of supplication. Even if this was the original significance, however, it is clear that according to the Genesis story they did it because they were ashamed. So also in Homer it appears that Odysseus' chief reason for covering himself with the branch was to hide his nakedness. For this reason too he asked Nausicaa for some clothing: see lines 178–9:

> ἄστυ δέ μοι δεῖξον, δὸς δὲ ῥάκος ἀμφιβαλέσθαι,
> εἴ τί που εἴλυμα σπείρων ἔχες ἐνθάδ᾿ ἰοῦσα.

the individual nudists, any more than a condemnation of gambling is a condemnation of individual bookmakers. If, however, a real sense of right and wrong does not exist, one cannot expect to find a real sense of shame. It is not, therefore, surprising to find unashamed nakedness in a society in which one may also find unashamed vice and crime of all kinds. Nudism today, as perhaps also in ancient Greece, is not a sign of moral progress, but rather a symptom of incipient moral decay. This is particularly true of nudity on the stage, and of the so-called "strip-tease", in which the interest of the spectator is directed not on the æsthetic beauty of the human form but on the sensual pleasure of the gradual undressing of the artiste. Thus the weak point in Dr. Havelock Ellis' argument in favour of nudism is the moral one; for his argument seems to degenerate into little better than a rhapsody on the strip-tease masquerading as a philosophical justification of the practice of nudity.[1] That unashamed nakedness may be a sign of a general moral decay is also borne out by the behaviour of certain prisoners of war of low moral character in the hands of the Japanese during the last war. I am informed that some such men, under the general strain imposed by living under the rigorous conditions which prevailed in the jungle, lost all sense of human dignity and propriety, and discarded with their clothing their sense of honesty and general decency. Others of a higher standard, even though outwardly freed from the fetters of conventional society, always retained at least a loincloth as a symbol, if of nothing else, at least of the fact that they were civilized men.

There is, however, another type of nudism—what we may call conscientious nudism—which cultivates nakedness for social, hygienic or religious reasons. The nudism of ancient Sparta may perhaps be placed in this class, and also a certain amount of modern naturism, though its apparent popular appeal—in theory if not in practice—cannot be attributed to this. And, incidentally, from the defensive attitude assumed in many of the articles in nudist magazines, it would seem

[1] See, *Sex in Relation to Society*, Chapter III, esp. pp. 71-4.

that they are as acutely conscious of nakedness as are other people. Even with this class of cultivated nakedness, as with the types discussed above, it may be that it is a sign of degeneration rather than of true progress. Certain religious sects, also, have attempted to discard clothing on principle, as they regard it, correctly, as a legacy of the Fall of Adam, and seek, incorrectly, to remove the cause of sin by removing its effect; as in a similar way the ancient Rechabites sought to avoid the evils of a settled, as opposed to a nomadic, life by living artificially in tents and abstaining from wine.

Apart from such conscious or unconscious types of habitual nakedness as have been mentioned above, it is generally true that to be seen naked by others is something which appears to most people either shameful or, to say the least, embarrassing —and particularly to be seen naked by members of the opposite sex. At any rate, this is certainly true of the Hebrew-Christian civilization in Europe, with which we are particularly concerned; and the implicit admiration of the state of unashamed nakedness, as in the writings of Milton,[1] is all the more noteworthy as it reveals the realization in the Christian mind of the inseparable association of the shame of nakedness and the sense of sin.

This feeling of shame, however, appears for several reasons to be wholly irrational. We are naturally born naked, as are the other animals, who, so far as we can tell from their behaviour, do not display a similar shame at their own nakedness. Furthermore, although it may seem strangely paradoxical, we may be fully conscious of the inherent purity and beauty of the human body as the creation of God and even admire it in works of art, and yet remain aware of the sense of shame. Indeed, the person who habitually displays in public what society considers to be too much of his (or her) body is reckoned to be either mentally unbalanced or completely shameless. It may, of course, be argued that this is only due to the conventions of society; but such a contention brings us no nearer to the real reason for this feeling of shamefulness, for all conventions have, at least in origin,

[1] See *Paradise Lost*, Book IV, 312-24.

66

some reason behind them. Such an argument merely states the problem in a different way: instead of, "Why are we ashamed of appearing naked?" it asks, "Why does convention frown upon nakedness?" The conventions of society are really nothing more than the general consensus of the opinions of individuals; to say that such-and-such a course of behaviour is merely a convention, is only to say that at some time most people decided to do it, and have decided to continue so.

Further, so far as we are consciously aware, this sense of shame is not really akin to the sense of guilt which afflicts us as the result of some moral lapse. Indeed, the resultant feeling may be similar; but if a man feels a sense of shame at being discovered naked, it seems, in a sense, to be an undeserved shame, since it may not arise as the result of a crime or sin committed. We are ashamed of nakedness, even though we may not be aware of any sin which makes us ashamed of it; and this appears to have been the case in Genesis, iii, where Adam and Eve are ashamed of their nakedness after a sin which apparently had nothing to do with it, and, moreover, which at the time had not been recognized as a sin.

3. *This Shame is of a Sexual Character*

This sense of shame is also reproduced in dreams, one of the most common of which is the embarrassment dream of nakedness. In considering the dream we may be better able to perceive the meaning of this feeling of shame than in considering the same feeling in our waking life; for though we may never have actually appeared in public insufficiently clad, yet the state of nakedness and its attendant embarrassment may occur frequently in dreams. It is, moreover, especially significant that it should occur in the dream when it does not occur in waking life—except, of course, in early infancy when we could appear naked before other persons and yet remain unashamed. It is significant for this reason: that if the content of our dreams is in any sense a recollection of previous experience or impressions, the dream of appearing naked can only be a recollection from the earliest infancy of either the individual or the race.[1] Furthermore, if the Psycho-analytic theory of dreams as wish-fulfilments is correct,[2] then the recurrence of nakedness in dreams can be explained in two complementary ways. First, it may be symbolic of something else which is desired by the dreamer. And, second, it may be due either to the unconscious desire to recover the feeling of unashamed nakedness which belonged to our first parents in the infancy of the race, or to an equally unconscious desire for a regaining of that delight in exhibiting one's own person experienced in the infancy of the individual. Both of these desires, which we assume still to exist in the civilized adult, because of their apparent fulfilment in dreams, are released from the unconscious by the partial breakdown of the psychic censorship in sleep, which, as has been mentioned already, preserves the peace of the Ego by keeping repressed in the unconscious system those desires and concepts which are repugnant to the conscious. But in the dream we are presented with the ambivalent emotions of a desire for, and a shame at, nakedness. The former is represented in the content of the dream by appearing naked, and the latter by the sensation of embarrassment which even the partial relaxation of the censor during sleep cannot wholly remove, or which, more accurately, represents the disapproval of the desire by the censorship. If this is so, then we may conclude that the sense of shame in the conscious mind is at once the cause and the outward sign of the repression of a desire for nakedness.

If this analysis of the manifest dream-content is correct, then we are presented with the question as to what this desire for nakedness symbolizes: in other words, what is the latent dream-content. This, however, does not present a great problem. The two complementary desires of nakedness—for being naked oneself, and for seeing others naked—which are two of the so-called component impulses of the sex-instinct, are both commonly observable in young children, and also appear among adults as the sexual perversions of Exhibitionism and Scoptophilia which are in fact regressions to an infantile attitude to life: and so we are led to believe that the

[1] See Freud: *Interp. of Dreams*, pp. 166 ff.   [2] Ibid., pp. 129 ff.

desire for nakedness is a manifestation of sexual desire. But the natural desires in the infant for expression of his sexual instinct are forbidden by external forces, by the parents and nurses of the child in particular, and by the conventions of society in general, and they are therefore driven underground and repressed in the unconscious because they are forbidden.[1] If this is so, and if, as Freud asserts, dreams of nakedness are exhibition dreams, then it would appear that in them the desire for nakedness returning from a state of repression during sleep must symbolize sexual desire.

We may also notice that the offence of indecent exposure of one's person usually involves the display of the sexual organs, and that the gravity of the offence is increased if a man commits it in the presence of women. Here there may be observed the almost unconscious connection made by society between nakedness and sexuality.

This connection is further illustrated in the thought of the ancient Hebrews. The Biblical word '*ĕrvāh—pudenda*—translated in the English versions "nakedness", is derived from the word '*ārāh* meaning "to be naked, or bare", which itself has not any specifically sexual connotation. The Lexicon[2] does not say whether the use of this word to mean the sexual organs is figurative or not; this point, however, is only of secondary importance; what is of interest is the connection in the word between nakedness and sex.

From what has been said above it may be seen that the connection between nakedness and the sexual instinct is not merely accidental, but shows a deep unconscious connection of the two ideas in human thought. If this is so then it is, I think, reasonable to suggest that the sense of shame at nakedness must be attributed to, and is an extension of, the apparently shameful character of Sex. And this leads us to the next stage of our study, to the consideration of why sexuality should be thought shameful.

[1] See further, Havelock Ellis: *Psychology of Sex*, pp. 159 ff.; Freud: *Interp. of Dreams*, pp. 236–41; *Introductory Lects.*, etc., pp. 275–6.
[2] Brown, Driver and Briggs: *Hebrew and English Lexicon of the Old Testament*, p. 788 (*b*).

4. *The Shameful Character of Sex*

Although we may fully realize that the sexual function and organs of the human body are in themselves merely a part of our human constitution as intrinsically pure and necessary as, for example, our digestive or respiratory systems, they carry in the mind of the ordinary person a sense of shamefulness and a vague impropriety which the other functions and organs of the body do not, except in so far as those other functions and organs may be connected physically or psychologically with the processes of reproduction.[1] But the sense of shamefulness associated with the actual organs of reproduction is really only an extension—we may almost say, a localization—of the sense of shame which belongs to the processes of reproduction, to the sexual function. Such a sense of shame, however, may be regarded today as largely conventional; but, as I have tried to point out above, convention is really nothing more than a general unwritten formulation of the opinions of individuals. If conventional society is shocked by "sex", it is only because individual members of society have been shocked by it in the past. In fact this connection between the sexual and the improper—one might almost say, the identification of the two—has been so strongly marked in human thought as to produce the teaching of both Christian and non-Christian ascetics who condemned all forms of sexual indulgence even in marriage as being immoral. Even Saint Augustine taught

> that inherited sinfulness consisted mainly in that concupiscence through which the race was propagated, since under the present conditions of a fallen world, marriage, in itself right and sinless, was inevitably accompanied by passions which are sinful.[2]

---

[1] Such a distinction into sexual and a-sexual parts of the body seems to be recognized in the New Testament: see 1 Corinthians, xii, 23-4. "And those members of the body, which we think to be less honourable, upon these we bestow more abundant honour; and our uncomely parts have more abundant comeliness. For our comely parts have no need: but God hath tempered the body together, having given more abundant honour to that part which lacked."

[2] E. J. Bicknell, in *Essays Catholic and Critical*, p. 214.

Teaching of this kind, though formally repudiated by the Church, has left a definite mark on its thought, and is undoubtedly the real basis for the popular idea that immorality is limited to sexual vice. Even a murderer, though recognized as a sinner, is not popularly called an immoral man.[1]

If therefore, in following ascetic teaching, we find sin in sexuality—that is the sin of concupiscence—we run the risk of falling into the puritanical error of considering pleasure in general as evil just because it is pleasurable. In fact, what is wrong, what really constitutes concupiscence, is not the normal sexual appetite or the proper gratification of it, but the misuse of the sexual impulse merely for the sake of procuring enjoyment; in the same way, it is wrong to be a glutton, but not wrong to feel hungry or to enjoy one's daily food. Moreover, it cannot be argued that sexual intercourse is of itself evil, since it is necessary for the purpose of reproduction; and the pleasure involved in it may be considered as necessary, to ensure that reproduction shall take place. Further, it is unthinkable that the Creator did not intend mankind to propagate itself, since otherwise he would not have created man with such powers and such an instinct if in every use of them they would prove to be occasions of sin. This, indeed, remains true even if the first sexual pleasure may be accidental and spontaneous—like Lamb's account of the discovery of roast pork—and subsequent sexual indulgence wrongly sought merely as a means of regaining that pleasure.

Nevertheless, taking all that has been said above into account, it remains true that

in the popular view . . . sexual is something which combines references to the differences of the sexes, to pleasurable excitement and gratification, to the reproductive function, and to the idea of impropriety and the need for concealment.[2]

[1] Compare Miss Dorothy Sayers' *The Other Six Deadly Sins*; and also, *Doctrine in the Church of England*, pp. 61–2.

[2] Freud: *Introductory Lects., etc.*, p. 256.

Thus it would appear that man feels two apparently irrational senses of shame—shame of nakedness and shame of sexuality—and further, that nakedness is considered shameful because sexuality is. If this reasoning is correct, then the sense of shame experienced by Adam and Eve at their own nakedness must also be regarded as shame of a sexual nature. This being so, we are presented in Genesis, iii, with two ideas which still seem to have no connection with one another, but which according to the apparent meaning of the Biblical narrative must be assumed to bear on one another—namely, the two ideas, (a) that the first sin was disobedience—"Hast thou eaten of the tree, whereof I commanded thee that thou shouldest not eat?"—and (b) that the result of that sin was a feeling of shame which is now seen to be of a sexual character—"And the eyes of them both were opened, and they knew that they were naked." If then the result of sin produced a sense of shame identifiable as of a sexual character, it is not unreasonable to suppose that the sin itself was of a similar character—in fact a sexual sin.

5. *A Sexual Cause of the Origin of Sin*

As we have had occasion to mention earlier, the theory of Psycho-analysis attributes the origin of the sense of guilt and therefore also of morality and religion to a sexual cause—to the Œdipus complex: that is, to the incestuous desires of the son towards the mother, and the murder of the father of the primitive horde in order to achieve this object. Though we may disagree with the Freudian theory on the grounds set out in the last chapter—namely, its implicit non-theistic presupposition—yet we cannot help but notice that both the Biblical account of the fall of Adam, and some of the Fathers of the Christian Church, see a definite connection between sexuality and the origin of sin and moral awareness. It is also noticeable that the individual's introduction to morality is through prohibitions of a sexual nature: the earliest activity forbidden to an infant is activity which in the infantile mind is connected either directly or indirectly with sexuality—

interest, that is, in the processes of nourishment and excretion[1] or in the actual organs of sex.[2]

Now when we remember that the Biblical narratives of the Creation and of the Fall have parallels in similar stories in other parts of the world, it is not perhaps surprising to observe that in some of these Fall myths a certain sexual element appears also. What is, however, remarkable is that in one of these stories recounted by Frazer this sexual element is very similar to the underlying *motif* of the Œdipus complex which forms the basis of Freud's theory. This folk-story, to account for the origin of death, is told by the natives of the Admiralty Islands.

> They say that once on a time there was an old woman, and she was frail. She had two sons, and they went a-fishing, while she herself went to bathe. She stripped off her wrinkled old skin and came forth as young as she had been long ago. When her sons came from the fishing they were astonished to see her. The one said, "It is our mother," but the other said, "She may be your mother, but she shall be my wife." Their mother overheard them and said: "What were you two saying?" The two said: "Nothing! We only said that you are our mother." "You are liars," she retorted, "I heard you both. If I had had my way, we should have grown to be old men and women, and then we should have cast our skin and been young men and young women. But you have had your way. We shall grow old men and old women, and then we shall die." With that she fetched her old skin, and put it on, and became an old woman again. As for us, her descendants, we grow up and we grow old. But if it had not been for those two young scapegraces, there would have been no end of our days, we should have lived for ever and ever.[3]

If this folk-story is subjected to an analysis similar to that applied to a dream, certain interesting facts may come to light. The two sons represent the divided natural impulses of

[1] Compare Freud: *Introductory Lects., etc.*, p. 268; *New Introductory Lects., etc.*, p. 131; Havelock Ellis: *Psychology of Sex*, p. 118.

[2] Compare Freud: *Introductory Lects., etc.*, pp. 262-3.

[3] Frazer: *Folk-Lore in the Old Testament* (Abridged Edition), pp. 28-9.

one individual, the one representing the infantile incestuous desire, and the other the desires of the developed personality under the guidance of the super-ego. The shedding of the old skin and the emergence of the mother as a young woman reveal a returned infantile memory of the mother as she was then. The whole appears as little more than a thinly veiled account of the endo-psychic conflict of the Œdipus type in the mind of the savage, which he recognizes as being wrong. To it, however, is ascribed the origin of the fate which awaits mankind, that is, death: and death, too, is the punishment meted out to Adam in the Biblical story, for he is driven away from the Tree of Life.

We must, however, remember that the myth as it appears in Genesis, iii, is not in its original form, but has been consciously recast to suit the theology of its adapter. What the original form of the story was as it was first told by the primitive Hebrews, or by the races from whom they heard it, we can only guess at by comparing the myths found in different parts of the Semitic world. But in view of what has been said above, we must be prepared to entertain the idea that it may well have connected sexuality with death more explicitly, since, also, Adam does not fall into sin until after the creation of the first woman, whose name, ḥǎvvāh—Eve—suggests, according to the etymology of Genesis, iii, 20, that in the myth she was perhaps thought of more as the mother of mankind than as the wife of Adam. Moreover, the later working over of the myth did not succeed in eradicating something which has been noted already—that Adam's sin resulted in a sense of shame of a sexual character. It is also perhaps tempting to suggest that the fruit offered by Eve to Adam is really symbolic and has some sexual significance: such a suggestion, indeed, is not as far-fetched as it may at first appear, for in the Old Testament there is already evidence of such erotic symbolism in the Song of Solomon.[1]

From these observations it may be noticed that not only in certain trends of Christian Theology and in Psycho-analysis,

[1] See ii, 16; iv, 12, 13; vi, 11; vii, 7, 8. Compare Freud: *Interp. of Dreams*, p. 330, and *Introductory Lects.*, etc., p. 131.

but also in primitive myth, a connection is made between sexuality on the one hand and the origin of sin and of the sense of morality on the other.

6. Pride as the Origin of Sin

Besides the sexual impulse, however, another thing is also connected with the primal sin of man; and this again, it should be observed, appears in various forms in the three separate sources in which the connection between sin and sexuality has been noticed.

Saint Augustine attributes the origin of sin to pride, both in the angels and in man.[1] In both places, he says, "initium omnis peccati est superbia", and in the second he describes pride as a "perverse desire of height, in forsaking Him to whom the soul ought solely to cleave, as the beginning thereof, to make the self seem the one beginning".[2] This sin of Pride—"the inordinate desire to excel" [3]—is regarded by Catholic moralists as the sin *par excellence*, the source and origin of all sin. When, therefore, in the light of Saint Augustine's definition, we realize that by pride we mean the desire for, and consequently also the pleasure in, the domination of others by the self, we may recognize in pride the dominant instinct of the Individual Psychology of Adler— the instinct of self-preservation, which, as it is essentially competitive, he has himself called the "power-instinct". For this instinct, when it comes into conflict with the same instinct to survive in another person, immediately becomes an aggressive impulse directed solely to the end of subduing and dominating the rival.

When speaking earlier of a possible sexual origin of sin, we had occasion to mention the Psycho-analytic theory which traces the sense of guilt and the origin of morals to the Œdipus complex. At this point, however, it is of interest to

[1] See *De Civitate Dei*, XII, vi, A, and XIV, xiii, A.
[2] *The City of God*, tr. John Healey (J. M. Dent & Co.), Part III, p. 30.
[3] Davis: *Moral and Pastoral Theology*, Vol. I, p. 236.

notice that there are, as it were, two aspects to that complex, the sexual and the aggressive, of which the former is directed towards the mother and the latter against the father. Thus in the great primeval crime which Freud supposes, it may be said that an aggressive instinct rather than a sexual one was manifested in the actual murder of the father of the father of the horde; and, as the sense of guilt is a result of this crime rather than a direct result of the incestuous desires of man, morality may be regarded as being consequent upon the exercise of an aggressive impulse, and only indirectly upon the exercise of a sexual impulse. In other words, although the sense of guilt, from which morality sprang, is according to this theory an indirect result of the incestuous desire of the sons for the mother, its immediate and direct cause was the aggressive act of murder—an expression of a desire to control and dominate the father which could only be attained at the cost of his life. For the present, however, our interest is centred not upon any real or apparent connection between the sexual and the aggressive impulse in man, but rather on the fundamental identity of the aggressive impulse with the feeling of pride. To sum up, we may notice that pride and the aggressive impulse have these two points in common: both are expressions of the desire for domination over others, and of the enjoyment of such domination, whether it exists in actual fact or only in the imagination; and both are in some way connected with the first crime or sin of humanity and with the origin of moral awareness.

This Pride-Aggression impulse may seem to have no real connection with the sin of Adam, which in the Fall myth in Genesis is clearly presented as a sin of disobedience. I would, however, venture to suggest that the idea of disobedience to a known command of God has been introduced into the original story by the writer of the Genesis account, and that he has done this because of his own experience of sin as a transgression of the Law and because, like all Jews, he regarded the Law as of permanent effect. A comparison of the story in Genesis with what we may call its parent myths may help to justify the view that the disobedience of Adam is not an original part of the myth of the Fall. The general theme of these primitive stories of the Fall of Man and the origin of death which have been gathered from different parts of the world and collected by Frazer in his work *Folk-Lore in the Old Testament*, is more or less uniform, though the actual forms of the myth vary considerably among different peoples. To speak thus of a general underlying theme is not to say that all Fall myths, and Creation myths like them, are ultimately to be derived from one original which by a process of analysis and comparison we can reconstruct, by a process that is analogous to textual criticism. Rather, I believe that though one particular form of the myth may have descended from another, they are to be regarded as ultimately independent and spontaneous growths among different peoples, like, for example, the theories held by children about reproduction. If they do in fact conform to a generally uniform pattern this is not to be regarded as a sign of their mutual dependence or their common ancestry, but rather of a uniform psychological outlook among the primitives of different parts of the world. It nevertheless remains true that we may construct a basic model of such stories, but in doing so we are not reconstructing their lost prototype, but rather making a composite picture out of their most common elements. By a careful comparison of the different versions, Frazer found it possible to produce what we may call, if not the original, at least a basic version of the story, which he outlines as follows:

The benevolent Creator, after modelling the first man and woman out of mud and animating them by the simple process of blowing into their mouths and noses, placed the happy pair in an earthly paradise, where, free from care and toil, they could live on the sweet fruits of a delightful garden and where birds and beasts frisked about them in fearless security. As a crowning mercy he planned for our first parents the great gift of immortality, but resolved to make them the arbiters of their own fate, by leaving them free to accept or reject the proffered boon. For that purpose he planted in the midst of the garden two wondrous trees that bore fruits of very different sorts, the fruit of the one being fraught with death to the eater, and the other with life eternal. Having done so, he sent the serpent to the man and woman, and charged him to deliver this message: "Eat not of the Tree of Death, for in the day ye eat thereof ye shall surely die; but eat of the Tree of Life and live for ever." Now the serpent was more subtle than any beast of the field, and on his way he bethought him of changing the message; so when he came to the happy garden and found the woman alone in it, he said to her, "Thus saith God: Eat not of the Tree of Life, for in the day ye eat thereof ye shall surely die; but eat of the Tree of Death, and live for ever." The foolish woman believed him, and ate of the fatal fruit, and gave of it to her husband, and he ate also. But the sly serpent himself ate of the Tree of Life. That is why men have been mortal and serpents immortal ever since, for serpents cast their skins every year and so renew their youth. If only the serpent had not perverted God's good message and deceived our first mother, we should have been immortal instead of the serpents; for like the serpents we should have cast our skins every year, and so renewed our youth perpetually.[1]

Comparing this with the Biblical narrative, Frazer later says:

The story of the Fall of Man in the third chapter of Genesis appears to be an abridged version of this savage myth . . . The principal, almost the only, omission, is the silence of the narrator as to the eating of the fruit of the tree of life by the serpent, and the consequent attainment of immortality by the reptile. Nor is it difficult to account for the lacuna. The vein of rationalism which runs through the Hebrew account of creation . . . could hardly fail to find a stumbling-block in the alleged immortality of serpents; and the redactor of the story in its final form has removed this stone of offence from the path of the faithful by the simple process of blotting out the incident entirely from the legend.[2]

If we consider the story of the Fall of Man in this form, which we may regard as a likely reconstruction of what the author of the Genesis version adapted, we may see in the eager eating of the forbidden fruit a determined, though misguided, attempt on the part of our first parents, to ensure immortality for themselves. The story of the Fall is in fact the record of man's attempt to gain for himself a superiority over

[1] Frazer: *Folk-Lore in the Old Testament* (Abridged Edition), p. 19.　　　　　　　　[2] Ibid., pp. 32–3.

78

other things and an equality with God. In this way, the many variants of the story of the perversion of God's message recounted by Frazer,[1] which led to the eating of the wrong fruit against the alleged wish of God, may be regarded as lame attempts by man not only to justify his failure to achieve, but also to gloss over his desire to obtain for himself, a coveted equality with God—namely, immortality and independence. There is a great deal of truth in popular proverbs, often revealing a deep psychological insight, and here we may call to mind the saying, *Qui s'excuse, s'accuse*, as being particularly appropriate. Primitive man's attempt to shift the responsibility for his failure to achieve independence and immortality on to the serpent, merely points more clearly to the desire for those qualities already existing in the mind of man. As Dr. Hadfield has put it so neatly: "Adam blamed Eve and Eve blamed the serpent, but God was not deceived, and drove *them* out of the garden." [2]

If by this analysis the real significance of the primitive myths of the Fall of Man has been revealed, then it would appear that the sin which the redactor of Genesis represents —or misrepresents—as a sin of disobedience is in reality the sin of pride: the sin of desiring superiority over one's fellow creatures and an equality with the Creator which does not truly belong to the creature.[3]

7. *Procreation and the Sense of Pride*

As has been noticed earlier, certain variants of the primitive myth of Man's Fall contain a sexual element. Among these perhaps may be included the parent version of the story of Adam and Eve, if the suggestion was correct that the fruit presented by Eve has a sexually symbolic meaning, and if we were right in supposing that their shame after their sin was of a sexual character. What precisely the significance of this

[1] Frazer: *Folk-Lore in the Old Testament* (Abridged Edition), pp. 20–6.   [2] *Psychology and Morals*, p. 46.
[3] This indeed is the real tragedy behind "*Frankenstein*" and Kapek's "R.U.R."—the repetition of the primal sin of man—the rebellion of the creature against the Creator.

sexual element is cannot be determined easily, since the unconscious formulation of the myth has taken care to disguise the real nature of the sinful desire which caused Man's Fall. It has been possible, however, by following one strand of evidence, to arrive at the conclusion that this desire was of the nature of a proud-aggressive impulse: a desire for equality with God, for immortality and independence. It now remained for us to see if this proud-aggressive impulse is in any way connected with the sexual impulse, and with the sense of shame which seems to arise from it.

The connection between what has been said above about the proud-aggressive impulse manifested in the form of a desire and what will be said below about its fulfilment through the exercise of the sexual impulse will perhaps be more easily followed if it is compared with something which occurs in the mental life of neurotics and children. This phenomenon is the replacement of a desire by an imagined reality—a wish-fulfilment fantasy. In neurotics this is frequently revealed in their obsessive acts and in children in their play and in their dreams.[1] In the childhood of the race we may see a similar substitution; in place of the unsatisfied desire for equality with God, there arose the more satisfying wish-fulfilment—the imagined feeling of such an equality.

In the procreative functioning of the sexual impulse we may see delegated to man some of the creative power of God. In this function man has a power which is common to all God's creatures, but with the difference that man is conscious of the possession of this power as something to be used by him, and over which he has a degree of control. In the rest of nature, on the other hand, the function is exercised either automatically or instinctively, as a reaction to the appropriate stimuli, but without the consciousness of it being a power over which they have control—that is, of course, so far as we are able to understand the psychology of animals in this respect. If indeed they have any such consciousness, then the whole question of an animal Fall is raised, which is outside

[1] See further Freud: *Introductory Lects., etc.*, pp. 221-3 and 308-12; *Interp. of Dreams*, pp. 133-7.

80

the scope of this present study. Observation of a domestic cat, however, leads me to believe that they seem to be wholly at the mercy of instinctual desires and to have little or no capacity for what Freud has called sublimation. At any rate, human beings, in the words of the Psalmist, have children at their desire, and, conversely, do not have children at their desire. The thought that may immediately come to our minds, that they also have children they do not desire, does not invalidate this observation; for what is really of significance is not whether man procreates or does not procreate as he desires, but whether he intends to do so or not to do so. In other words man appears to have a greater degree of choice in the exercise of his sexual function than do the other animals. He is in this respect more his own master than the brute creation, in so far as his actions, if not also his desires, can be controlled by his will, which has a greater control over his instincts than the animals have over theirs. For strong as is the sex instinct in man, it is not so strong as to be completely uncontrollable. Now I would suggest that this difference between man and the animals was observable by man before the Fall, and that it was a contributory cause of the feeling of pride in man.[1] It may be argued that this idea of man possessing a sense of superiority over the animal creation is contradicted by the ideas of Totemistic man about his kinship with the animals. But, as I hope to show later, the phenomena of Totemism are to be understood as symptoms of a spiritual degeneration of man; and that therefore totemistic beliefs cannot necessarily be assigned to man as he was before the Fall. Further, though belief in kinship with the animals formed part of totemistic theory, this is not by

[1] It is possible that the realization by primitive man of his ability to control his own procreative activity lies at the root of early agricultural fertility cults, with their emphasis on the phallic symbols and sympathetic magic, rather than a belief that by such rites and ceremonies he could control and direct so-called demonic powers, which belong to a stage of human development after the Fall. Magic is mechanical rather than religious or spiritual, and man's control of the reproductive activity of nature is thus only an extension of his control of human reproduction.

any means the same as saying that man at that time was unaware of his real difference from the animals. Though this may seem inconsistent, it is no more so than later belief, as is illustrated in the Biblical myth of the Creation and Fall, in which the ideas of the apparent inferiority of the animals to man, and of their equality to him, both find a place.[1]

Further, as man is consciously aware of the exercise of his will as the controlling agent in his actions, he is not only aware of a superiority to the rest of creation, but he can also see in himself a reflection, as it were, of God, whose actions are controlled by his divine will. In other words, man realized that he was in the image of God, and that in the freedom of a creative will he bore the likeness of divinity. As God can create or not create according as he wills, so too man can use his (delegated) power to (pro-)create or not to (pro-)create according to his own will. In this sense, therefore, limited though it may be, through his ability to generate offspring, man became aware of the apparent fulfilment of his desires for equality with God and superiority over other creatures whose sexual and reproductive behaviour appeared to him to be more spontaneous and less subject to psychic control than his own. From this sense of seeming equality in creative activity, coupled with the idea of immortality, through his children—a perpetuation of his own kind—there also arose a sense of self-sufficiency, of independence of God, and the thought, albeit unexpressed, that children, so far from being heritage and gift that cometh of the Lord, were his own, his very own, creation. If this analysis is correct, the feeling of pride in man, which has been defined above as the desire for, and the enjoyment of, an either real or imagined sense of equality with God, and to which the origin of sin has been attributed, may in fact issue from the exercise of the sexual function in man: or, alternatively—though this is

[1] Compare Genesis, ii, 19–20, with iii, 1–5. "And out of the ground the Lord God formed every beast of the field, and every fowl of the air . . . but for Adam there was not found an helpmeet for him." This should be contrasted with the way in which the Serpent and the Woman are able to converse freely in iii.

really only a different way of looking at the same thing—the proud-aggressive impulse found a means of expression, of satisfying its desires for independence and immortality, in the exercise of the sexual instinct, by what really amounted to a wish-fulfilment fantasy. The idea of being able to exist and to produce children in apparently complete independence of God, although it does not necessarily arise from, nor give rise to, the exercise of the sexual instinct, may yet be regarded as the cause or the result of the feeling of pride in man, particularly when we consider that through his children primitive man also feels himself to be immortalized.[1] This may seem to be a paradoxical equation of cause and effect; but in fact Psycho-analytic experience teaches that in the primitive the two instincts of sex and aggression are virtually undifferentiated,[2] so that to speak of cause and effect in this context, though it may seem more convenient to do so, is perhaps to look for a distinction into two separate impulses of one sexual-aggressive instinct which cannot really be made. If this is so, then it would appear that the link may have been found which connects the two divergent strands of ideas attributing the origin of sin to pride and to sexuality respectively.

This is perhaps a convenient place to digress from the main argument, in order to round off the discussion of what led to the formulation of the Fall myth in its present shape in Genesis. The substitution of the Tree of the Knowledge of Good and Evil for the Tree of Death may be more fully

[1] This belief seems to be born out in certain parts of the world by the practice of killing the first-born. "It is often believed that the father is re-born in his child; for this reason, at Tahiti and elsewhere, a chief should abdicate when a son is born (G.B., iv, 190); hence the infant is put to death. The birth of a son may be an indication that the father will die (the Baganda, FOT., i, 562). Again, because the son is in some way his father over again, the father's name must not be given to the first-born, and in Morocco the son is never called by the name of his father (if alive), unless that name be Mohammed"—S. A. Cook in *The Religion of the Semites*, pp. 688-9.

[2] See Freud: *Moses and Monotheism*, pp. 119-20.

understood in the light of what has been said above. When the Hebrew editor of the primitive myth came to revise it for his own purposes with the knowledge of the mortality of all creatures, he would have to find some other distinguishing feature between man on the one hand and the serpent on the other. It is not, I feel, sufficient to say, as Frazer does, that the redactor of Genesis merely omitted any reference to the alleged immortality of serpents. It is not perhaps crediting him with a sense of moral responsibility too much in advance of his age, to suggest that he saw a more significant distinction: that it was in the moral character of human behaviour that the main difference between man and the beasts chiefly lay, and for this reason the fruit which Adam and Eve ate is represented not as being of the tree of death, but of the tree of the knowledge of good and evil—the tree, that is, not of knowledge in its ordinary sense, but of morality.[1] Looking at the sin of Adam from the point of view of a person with a moral conscience influenced by a written code of law, he would see that sin as the transgression of a moral command, as, indeed, he realized his own sins to be. In fact, however, the conscious knowledge of morality does not precede sin, but follows it; morality is not the cause of sin (in the sense of wrong-doing), but rather its result, for where there is no sin, there are no qualms of conscience. The act done in ignorance may only appear as sinful (that is as causing a sense of guilt) when its performance has revealed its true character to be evil. "It is only if we are evil that we can be conscience stricken," writes Dr. Hadfield.[2] The uneasy conscience, which is the immediate source of human law, is the result of the evil act, even though that act when first committed was not a sin in the sense of being a transgression of such a known command. Thus Saint Paul, we may say, *appears* to be correct only in a limited

[1] Such a view of the work of the redactor of the Genesis myth is, I believe, quite consistent with the presence of very primitive elements in the narrative: it appears to have been his object to introduce his own interpretation, while altering the form of the myth as little as possible.

[2] *Psychology and Morals*, p. 44.

sense, that is, in so far as he speaks as a sinner, when he says, "I had not known sin, except through the law: for I had not known coveting, except the law had said, Thou shalt not covet." [1] Such a view makes clearer the Pauline idea that the real function of law, and of morality in general, is not so much to prevent men from sinning, which it in fact does not do, but to convince men of sin after the evil act has been committed. Thus in one sense sin, that is, an evil act committed by man, precedes morality; but in another sense sin, as the performance of an act which gives rise to a sense of guilt, must come after morality.

In the primitive mind, however, it is true to say that cause and effect are not clearly distinguished.[2] For this reason the writer of the story in Genesis has provided a command, not to eat the fruit of the tree of knowledge of good and evil, which appears to be absent from the parent version. The act of Adam, which caused his fall from innocence, is visualized as a breach of this command, whereas in fact the act came first and the uneasy conscience followed. Paradoxical though it may seem, there was no consciously known law forbidding Adam's "sin", until after the performance of that sin had shown it to be a breach of the absolute moral law.

This is perhaps of greater significance than we may have thought, when we remember what the Fathers of the Church have conceived to be the first sin of man. Pride, unlike the eating of a forbidden fruit, is not a breach of a known law, nor the result of an external temptation: but it arises more or less spontaneously in the mind of the sinner. It is not until this sin has actually been committed, that one realizes that there was such a sin to commit: and then it is revealed as the sins of idolatry and covetousness. That is to say, the sense of morality, which really corresponds with the Divine Law, is latent in the human mind, and is called forth by the sinful act,

[1] Romans, vii, 7 (R.V.).
[2] This is true to a certain extent of people today, and this simple-minded attitude is well illustrated by Stephen Leacock's satire: thus "Cholera is caused by a frightful pain in the stomach, and diphtheria is caused by trying to cure a sore throat" (*Literary Lapses*, Penguin Edition, p. 32).

but not created by it, as may appear to be the idea put forward by Freud in his exposition of the origin of morality. I have called this sense of morality "latent," but in doing so I do not intend this to be confused with the idea of repression. If it is to be located in any part of man's psychic system, it would belong rather to the preconscious than to the unconscious: if it answers to any psychological function previously defined elsewhere, it corresponds to that which is revealed in the sinner as conscience rather than to the super-ego of the Psycho-analyst. Here again we may see the difference of presupposition between Religion and Science, between the theocentric and anthropocentric views of life. The super-ego in one of its functions appears to be the counterpart of the conscience [1] but differs from it in this important respect, that it is a concept employed to explain the moral consciousness without reference to supernatural law or to absolute values of goodness and truth, upon which the Christian idea of the conscience really depends. If, however, we accept the religious belief that all things ultimately depend on God, then we may accept the idea of the super-ego as being part of the psychological mechanism of man ordained to fulfil its own purpose in man's life, in the same way as we recognize parents and educators to be the ministers of God in the upbringing and care of children. We must not, however, fall into the common error of thinking that, if we understand the mechanism of a psychical, as of a physical, process, we then know about it all there is to know. It is in this respect that the Freudian idea of the super-ego is deficient; while it regards the moral law by which the individual is warned and chastized as an internalization of an external law, it does not satisfactorily explain why such external laws arose in the minds of the first parents and educators. In other words, my own super-ego is alleged to be an internalization of the teaching of my parents, which was itself conditioned by the influence of their super-ego.[2] This process would appear to stretch back to infinity, but in

[1] Compare Freud: *New Introductory Lects.*, etc., pp. 81–2; *Group Psychology*, etc., pp. 68–9.
[2] See Freud: *New Introductory Lects.*, etc., pp. 84–5.

86

fact it does not. Accepting even the most thorough-going evolutionary theory, there must have been a first human being, or group of humans, who were sufficiently different from their animal ancestors to constitute a new species. The Freudian theory forces us to ask what it was that formed the super-ego of this first human species, or alternatively who were its educators. Religious belief, as I have endeavoured to define it, asserts divine influence as its origin and its educator, in the form of a latent moral awareness, which in the course of man's life was called into consciousness by sin. According to this view, therefore, if we presuppose the existence of God, we may also assume a divine law in the mind of man from the beginning.[1] The expulsion, then, from Eden, from primitive innocence is consequent upon the imagined fulfilment of man's desires—consequent, that is, upon his awareness of apparent equality with God including within it the fantasies of the fulfilment of both man's wishes, for immortality and for independence. "And the Lord God said, Behold, the man is become one of us, to know good and evil." [2] Man had become aware of, and found pleasure in, an apparent equality with God, which may be regarded as evil or as good: as evil, when it results in rebellion and thus reveals itself as pride, the sin of the man who gives not God the glory; as good, in so far as man realizes a proper sense of his independence, and there-fore also of his dependence on and responsibility towards God, and can say of all he seems to do himself, "Not unto us, O Lord, not unto us, but unto thy name give the praise." [3] But by a misuse of this apparent independence, and with it the realization of pride within the conscious mind, the primeval glory of Eden departed, and man, expelled from Paradise, himself set in their place the Cherubims and the fiery sword preventing his return to innocence.

[1] Compare Romans, ii, 14–15. "For when the Gentiles, which have not the law, do by nature the things contained in the law, these, having not the law, are a law unto themselves; which shew the work of the law written in their hearts, their conscience also bearing witness, and their thoughts the meanwhile accusing or else excusing one another."

[2] Genesis, iii, 22.   [3] Psalm, cxv, 1.

Thus the desire of man for immortality and for complete independence of God, which found its fantasy-fulfilment in the consciousness of being able to exercise a freedom of the will in the procreation of offspring, has haunted and blighted humanity ever since. Not only is it the first example of human pride and the origin of human sin, but it has also left a stigma upon all sex relations ever since, and is, I would suggest, the cause of the ambivalent feelings of repugnance and attraction which the idea of sexuality arouses in the mind of man.

8. *Examples of the Connection of the Sex and Power Instincts*

At this point we may notice that the connection between the sexual instinct and the aggressive power instinct is also illustrated in the laws and customs governing the relations of man and wife in society. It is significant that in patriarchal times, if not in the modern world, the husband is the master, the *bă'ăl*, of the wife, who is dependent on him for her whole livelihood, and over whom he has an authority not shared by others. Conversely, in popular language, a man's paramour, upon whose will and pleasure the man depends for any sexual gratification derived from her, is known as his mistress. This indeed may be a remote survival of the earlier form of marriage which was at the basis of matriarchy, but which later degenerated into prostitution.[1]

Again we may see this connection in the sexual perversions of Sadism and Masochism, the complementary feelings of sexual pleasure in inflicting and suffering pain respectively. Here in the aggressive impulses of the sexual instinct, which are physical manifestations of the mental desire for dominating the beloved object and of the complementary desire for being dominated by the beloved one, the connection of the two instincts is particularly interesting for our study of the infancy of the human race, as Freud has identified these perversions as regressions to an infantile attitude of mind. We

[1] Compare, Havelock Ellis: *Sex in Relation to Society*, p. 238; Robertson Smith: *Kinship and Marriage*, esp. pp. 191 ff.

may even go so far as to say that apart from the purely sensual and reproductive impulse of the sex-instinct—that is, those directed towards sexual intercourse—the most dominant component impulse is the aggressive one, the impulse to dominate and to excel.[1]

This connection is also revealed in a place where we may not have expected to find it, but where it leads straight to the mark at which we have been aiming. In the writings of Saint Paul we find a word which well expresses the aggressive nature of pride—πλεονεξία, which is perhaps more pregnant in meaning than the word "covetousness" by which it is translated in the English versions. The meaning given in the Lexicon[2] is "a greedy desire to have more", and though it is often synonymous with greed for wordly wealth, yet its association with the sins of the flesh, as in Colossians, iii, 5,[3] appears to give it a more general meaning, such as the word ἐπιθυμία also has, which occurs with πλεονεξία in the passage cited. Such a desire for more, a manifestation of the aggressive impulse which we have seen to be a component of the sex-instinct, makes it a significant word to group with fornication and fleshly lust. What is, however, of greatest importance for our present study is Saint Paul's use of πλεονεξία in his definition of it—and perhaps of the words with it—ἥτις ἐστὶν εἰδωλολατρεία : the sin of setting up a false god to be worshipped in place of the Creator.

9. Conclusion: Identity of Pride and Concupiscence

As the argument has covered rather a wide field with numerous digressions and illustrations, it may be useful to give here a short summary of the main steps, before we come

---

[1] See Freud: Introductory Lects., etc., pp. 261, 267; Havelock Ellis: Psychology of Sex, pp. 76, 170.

[2] Grimm-Thayer: Greek-English Lexicon of the New Testament, p. 516 a.

[3] Νεκρώσατε οὖν τὰ μέλη τὰ ἐπὶ τῆς γῆς, πορνείαν, ἀκαθαρσίαν, πάθος, ἐπιθυμίαν κακήν, καὶ τὴν πλεονεξίαν, ἥτις ἐστὶν εἰδωλολατρεία, . . .

to a conclusion. The essential stages in the argument, which for the sake of brevity will be stated here quite dogmatically, are as follows. Two apparently incompatible and unconnected theories have been put forward by Christians on the subject of human sin: the one assigned the cause of Man's fall to pride; the other regards concupiscence as the cause of the transmission of sin from one generation to another. The Genesis story of the Fall makes the first result of man's sin the realization of his nakedness. By an analytical interpretation of this myth, it has been suggested that what is presented in Genesis as a sin of disobedience results in shame of a sexual nature, of which the real cause is not direct disobedience, but rather the desire for equality with God finding an imagined fulfilment in the procreative functioning of the sex-instinct. This instinct in its normal and abnormal manifestations is closely linked with man's self-assertive and proud impulses, which may find a means of expression through sexuality, thus forming a unified sexual-aggressive impulse which, if it intrudes into man's relations with his Creator, is immediately revealed as the sin of idolatry.

From what has been said above—if it is correct—it would appear that the sense of shame associated with sexual matters is a feeling which is not really connected with sex itself, but is rather the displacement of the sense of guilt arising from pride on to sex; and that therefore the real sin of concupiscence is not properly the sin of taking pleasure in the normal exercise of the sexual function (which is really no more a sin than enjoying one's food), but rather it is the sin of pride which indirectly results from it or is expressed in it. Such a substitution of a secondary reason for an original one which is repugnant to the conscious Ego is not as far-fetched as it may appear. Theodor Reik, for example, has shown how such a process has changed the meaning of the savage custom of Couvade.[1] In a similar way, in many heathen customs which have persisted into Christian times, the original (heathen) meaning of the custom has been forgotten or intentionally

[1] See *Ritual: Psycho-Analytic Studies*, pp. 27 ff.

repressed, and another (Christian) reason has been sub-stituted.[1] In the present instance the association of guilt with pride has been intentionally repressed as being unwelcome to the conscious self; and a new and irrational guilt-association has been substituted—an association of guilt with sexuality in general, which was an appropriate scape-goat for pride, since pride had found its expression through sex.

In this way, therefore, Saint Augustine is right in pointing out that procreation does not take place without sin; but it is not the sin of concupiscence, but of pride, the guilt of the latter having been displaced on to the former.[2] But the rigidly ascetic teaching which appears to be a logical deduction from this is wrong, because it depends on a confusion of thought, and sees the basic sin not in the psychical pleasure of pride, but in the physical pleasure of sexual gratification. We may thus arrive at a synthesis of the two apparently incompatible views of the origin of sin: for pride and concupiscence are both expressions of the desires of man for equality with God finding expression in the exercise of the sexual instincts. So by the aid of an analytic study of material from various sources we have come to two conclusions, to which we looked forward at the beginning: first that the great primeval sin of man was a sin against God, and not, as Freud would persuade us, a crime against humanity; and second that the difference between the two ideas of the origin and transmission of sin found in the Fathers is more apparent than real, since the sin which manifests itself as either pride or concupiscence is at

[1] E.g., the Roman feast of Lupercalia, which was changed by Bishop Gelasius in A.D. 494 into the Feast of the Purification; and the use of holly and ivy as Christmas decorations; or the custom of "Egg-rolling" at Easter in the north of England, which is supposed to symbolize the rolling away of the stone from the sepulchre, but which is doubtless a heathen ceremony whose original significance has been suppressed.
[2] This must not be taken as an implied justification of sexual licence; true sexual morality depends upon other considerations. But it is, incidentally, a plea for common sense with regard to sex in general.

the bottom the sin of idolatry—the sin of putting man in the place of God as the ruling power in the world, the sin of worshipping and serving the creature more than the Creator, who is blessed for ever. Amen.

THE UNIVERSAL NEUROSIS AND THE DIVINE PSYCHIATRY

1. *Introductory: The Reaction of Man to Sin: Defence*

IN the last chapter it was suggested that the origin of sin in man is to be traced back to pride, to a desire for equality with God; and that this desire, which from its very nature cannot be fulfilled in fact, achieved an imagined fulfilment in fantasy, in the belief that through a certain natural function man had obtained the object of his wishes. This natural function was the sexual instinct, which appeared to gratify man's desire by giving him an illusion of creative power through his ability to procreate children, and an illusion of immortality through his offspring. If we isolate the aggressive-proud instinct from the sexual instinct, it would appear that the latter had been made the servant of the former; or, looked at in another way, that the desire for equality with God had arisen from the exercise of man's sexuality. Which came first, however, it seems impossible to decide, for the two are in fact inextricably mingled. In one sense, therefore, the problem of human sin is no nearer to solution as a result of this identification. We can only say that sin resulted from a mis-use of man's free will, of his freedom, that is, of desire as well as of action. It does not enable us to say why in the first place sin should have entered into the world and so have entailed so much suffering and misery in subsequent genera-tions. It does not make any more reasonable to the irreligious the apparent paradox of a good Creator and a sinful creation. This, however, was not the purpose for which it was written; if we may use an analogy from the study of medicine, it was intended rather as a diagnosis of the disease, than as a state-ment of the origin of the virus causing the disease. It may, it is true, be more interesting to know the "why" than the "how". But to know the latter is sufficient for practical pur-poses and is as far as scientific study can take us. To say why man chose to sin must remain a matter of speculation: and this can serve no practically useful purpose, as we cannot, so to speak, put back the clock to the time of Adam's innocence. Our study must, therefore, proceed from the point where we find Adam cast out of Paradise and prevented from returning to that primitive bliss by the flaming sword.

Considered from a psychological point of view this first result of sin in Adam—the expulsion from Eden—was a separation between the conscious (preconscious) and unconscious systems, and the establishment of a psychic barrier between them. Or rather, I would suggest that the emergence of the unconscious, in the Freudian sense, was actually caused by sin, and that the unconscious was, as it were, untenanted, when as yet man had not sinned against God. The real difference between the preconscious and the unconscious systems lies in the fact that the contents of the former are readily accessible to the conscious mind, whereas the contents of the latter are in a state of repression and therefore inaccessible. Such concepts as are thus repressed in the unconscious are repressed because they are unwelcome or repugnant to the conscious ego, and they are therefore held in prison in the unconscious by the super-ego, which thus acts as the protector of the peace of the ego, and the gaoler of the unwelcome thoughts. If such a view of the work of the super-ego is permissible, it will appear to combine the functions of a mental policeman and warder. Now in a city or state, if there were no crime and no criminals, the prisons would be empty and the police force (so far as it was concerned with the prevention of crime) unemployed and superfluous. We may perhaps press this analogy even further, if we remember that it is only an analogy; before the emergence of crime the policemen will be there potentially as citizens, and the stones out of which the prison will be built will exist elsewhere, in the quarry. If we apply this analogy to the mental life of man, we shall see that such was the happy state of humanity before sin broke in upon paradise. Before the Fall of Adam, there were no thoughts or desires which were permanently repugnant to his conscious mind, and so there was no need of

94

repression. Any thought or desire which was not actually conscious would remain not in the unconscious system in a state of repression, but only at a preconscious level, available when required. In this way we believe that man knew God, in the Biblical phrase, face to face: that is to say, intercourse with God was possible consciously, whereas among men in a state of sin such conscious intercourse with God is impossible. The sin of Adam produced in his conscious mind a sense of guilt as a result of the awakening of the moral consciousness which had previously been latent in man. This sense of guilt proved to be the first unwelcome inhabitant of man's conscious mind, and in order to preserve the peace of the ego, man endeavoured to thrust it away from consciousness, to forget it.

But such a course, though it may appear a desirable one, must prove impracticable for man so long as he still retains the knowledge of God in his conscious mind; for this knowledge is a constant reminder of the sin of man, of the desire for equality with God, which was what man really needed to forget. So long as the knowledge of God remained, there could be no peace of mind, and so it was necessary for this to be subjected to repression in the unconscious. If this is done, a double object is achieved: the unwelcome sense of guilt loses its force since the "victim" of the crime is in a sense removed; and also man achieved the object of his desire, superiority, by thus denying in his conscious mind the existence of his rival, and also paradoxically the secondary object of his desire, to forget his desire, as the person against whom that sinful desire was directed is forgotten. Thus man may be said to have forgotten God because he wished to forget him. He turned his back upon him because he did not want to see him, as we turn from some unpleasant or disgusting sight, or "close our eyes" to some undesired fact. In this way it may be said that man separated himself from God, and himself set in their place the fiery sword and the cherubim preventing his return to Eden. This may seem rather too speculative a reconstruction of man's first reaction to the consequences of his sin; but we may see an analogy in individual psychology,

95

in what Freud called the Psychopathology of Everyday Life, in the forgetting of the names of places and persons, the failure to carry out engagements or resolutions and the mislaying or damaging of objects. According to the Psychoanalytic interpretation of such apparent lapses of memory and accidents, they are by no means fortuitous but are in fact intentional, since, for example, the name of the person forgotten arouses unwelcome unconscious associations which have themselves arisen as a result of a formerly conscious wish associated with the now forgotten name; since these ideas are unwelcome the name which is associated with them is repressed or dissociated from them.[1] In man's forgetting of God I believe that we may see a similar process taking place. The knowledge of God gives rise both to man's desire against God, and to the reappearance of the unwelcome sense of guilt, and so man endeavours to thrust that knowledge out of his conscious system.

The uneasy conscience of man could not, however, find such a means of escape from reality so easily. An idea cannot simply be forgotten because we want to forget it; indeed, a conscious effort to forget often defeats its own object. The rational nature of our mental processes demands some reason for it to be forgotten, and so another process may be discerned in the mind of fallen man justifying his forgetting of God. The end of this process was the idea of the wrath of God. It is perhaps unnecessary to adduce any psychological evidence for the fact too often unrealized that, if a person commits some wrong against his neighbour, he feels after the event a hatred for his neighbour even greater than he had felt before it. As such a feeling of hostility is really quite unjustifiable, since if anyone should be hostile it is not the person who committed the crime, but the person against whom it was committed, it may be wondered why this feeling should arise at all. If the offended party should show any signs of resentment or hatred, the mind of the offender will be satis-

[1] See further, Freud: *Psychopathology of Everyday Life,* and *Introductory Lects., etc.,* Part I. Compare also the case of Extensive Amnesia in W. Brown: *Psychology and Psychotherapy,* pp. 50–5.

fied, for such an attitude on the part of his victim will seem to justify his crime. If on the other hand this does not happen, the crime will appear to be unjustified, and to remedy this a two-fold process must take place in the mind of the offender. In order to justify his action he must increase his own hatred of his victim, which in its turn must be justified and reinforced by an assumed hostility against the offender by the offended. A clear example of such a process may be seen in the propaganda of one country against another immediately before a war. The aggressor assumes a threat to himself on the part of his destined victim, which both fortifies his own resolves and justifies his aggression in his own eyes. A similar process appears in the behaviour of those individuals who, for example, justify their non-attendance at divine worship because some beloved person has died. Their usual argument is that they cannot believe in God if he has taken away their son (or mother, or whomsoever it may be). Leaving aside any question of the illogicality of such an argument, which in fact implies belief in God, it is easy to see that the reason they allege is only a reinforcement of an attitude of mind they possessed already. Although it appears rational to them, it is not really a reason but an unconsciously constructed excuse for their behaviour, since if they had previously believed in God their belief would not have been changed to hostility by their misfortune. Their later unbelief implies a previous hostility which is now justified by their idea of God's hatred of them.

Such a process of self-justifying hatred for God may well have gone on in the mind of primitive man. In order to make logical, and so possible, the forgetting (repression) of his knowledge of God, man constructed as it were the idea of God's anger against him, which seemed to justify not only his rebellion against God, but also his own attitude to God afterwards. The idea of God thus became repugnant to man for a variety of reasons, and was therefore repressed and forgotten; and in this way peace was restored to man's ego. At least, it seemed to be restored, but the relief was in fact only temporary, for the unwished for ideas of guilt, of the desire against God, and of the knowledge of God were not destroyed but only driven underground, confined in the unconscious.

It may at this point be convenient to compare what has been said above with the Freudian view of man's prehistory and of the origin of religion. In tracing the latter to the Œdipus complex, Freud noticed the similarity in causation and development with the obsessional neurosis. As our object here is also to trace the origin and development of religion, it is significant to observe that the analogy with the ætiology of the obsessional neurosis still holds good. Before the actual outbreak of the neurosis in the form of obsessive symptoms Freud notices three stages of development—early trauma, defence, and a period of latency. Now if the analysis given above of man's rebellion against God and its immediate results is correct, and if the Freudian analogy is valid, then these three stages ought to be observable. It need not, therefore, occasion any surprise if it is suggested that the sin of Adam, which has been defined as a sexual-aggressive act of the will against God, constitutes the trauma, and that this stage of defence is to be seen in the resultant hatred of God and the repression of the knowledge of God, and, with that knowledge, the repression of the desire against God and the sense of guilt. As in the Freudian theory the period of latency may be reasonably assumed as a consequence of the repression of the feelings of desire and guilt, and, with the presupposition of belief in the existence of God, of the knowledge of God. This latency is assumed this far: no exact date can be given of the origin of the first religion, and no date either for what we call the Fall of Man; but we are, I think, justified in assuming a considerable interval between them—a period in which religious thought, if we may so call it, found expression in animistic beliefs.[1]

---

[1] This is not the place to enter into a discussion of the origin and nature of animism: all I would say here is that it hardly merits the epithet of religious, since, if it acknowledges the supernatural, its believers cannot in any true sense be called worshippers. Its origins are probably to be traced to ideas about purely natural phenomena, the explanation of which was beyond the capacity of primitive man.

2. *The Origin of Religion as the Outbreak of the Neurosis*

Still following the Psycho-analytic analogy we must now expect to find an "outbreak of the neurosis", or in other words a beginning of religion as a system of ceremonial acts and prohibitive rules of no apparent meaning but with a force compelling them to be observed. If the discoveries of the comparative study of religion are to be accepted this "outbreak" of religion is to be found in Totemism, which appears to be the earliest phenomenon which can really be called religious.

In his book *Totem and Taboo* Freud has traced the origin of Totemism to the murder of the father of the primitive horde by his sons. This view, however, cannot be accepted as it stands, since in the argument up to this point it has been suggested, according to the presupposition of belief in God, that the first sin of man was an act against God, not one against his fellow men. Indeed, it may be added here, it is upon this belief in God that morality really depends. All sin is, in the last resort, against God; or, in other words, without God sin ceases to have any real meaning, and becomes impossible. For without belief in God and therefore in an absolute standard of morality, good itself ceases to be an absolute entity, and good and evil become only comparative and relative values of the same thing; the good of one man becomes the evil of another, and vice versa. With a belief in an absolute standard of good this cannot be, for if anything is evil for one person it cannot really be good for another, because what is evil cannot at the same time be regarded as absolutely good. This simple fact is, however, obscured by the generally loose usage of the term "good" to mean not only what may be beneficial to a particular person (and also perhaps detrimental to another), but also good in the absolute sense. Without belief in an absolute moral standard such absolute good loses its reality, and selfishness, the seeking of the personally beneficial rather than the truly good, becomes the only law. In such a state man can only sin against himself, by neglecting what is his own (relative) good; and love of one's neighbour, the seeking of his good without any ulterior motive, becomes mere folly. If then the absolute standard of morality, which depends on the existence of a moral God, is denied, it seems impossible to maintain a belief in human morality as anything more than a thinly veiled self-seeking. The existence of conscience, therefore, and of a real sense of guilt must also appear nonsensical unless they depend on an absolute standard of good which the evil act is seen to transgress. The first sin of man was an offence against absolute morality, and not merely a relatively good act (from the selfish point of view) which was branded as evil because it failed, like the liberating misdeed of which Freud speaks.

It is therefore suggested that if the events described by Freud as taking place in the remote prehistory of man actually took place, then, as they do not constitute a sufficient cause for the origin of the sense of guilt, it is not to them but to something even earlier that the real origin of the sense of guilt is to be traced. This, as has been pointed out above, is to be found in the sexual-aggressive act of the human will in desiring an equality with God, an act which Christian theology has long recognized as the sin of pride. Moreover, the argument which Freud adduces for the origin of totemistic belief as a conscious renunciation of instinctual desires, and the apparently conscious acceptance of the totem animal as a father-substitute, do not seem sufficient causes of the obsessive character of religious belief. More must be said later of the meaning and significance of the social reorganization following the murder of the father of the primeval horde; it is sufficient for the moment to notice that we must look for the underlying meaning of Totemism in something else—namely, in man's sin against God.

The task now presenting itself is to examine, and if possible to explain, in terms of man's sin against his Creator, rather than of the Œdipus complex, the unconscious origin of the rites and ceremonies of totemistic religion, on the analogy of the formation and outbreak of the symptoms of an obsessional neurosis. In other words, this study must move forward in order to demonstrate how the first religion worthy of the name depends not on the alleged murder of a human father, but on the deposition of the eternal God from his position of authority through the pride of man.

3. *The Interpretation of Obsessive Symptoms*

Something ought to be said at this point on the subject of the Psycho-analytic interpretation of the symptoms manifested by an individual suffering from an obsessional neurosis. This has, however, already been done by others more competent to do so from a purely medical point of view. Moreover, any brief survey here would doubtless prove either inadequate for those ignorant of the subject, or superfluous for those who have read and digested the works of Freud or others on the purely clinical aspects of Psycho-analysis. I shall therefore limit myself to giving a short account of one case, taken from Freud's *Introductory Lectures on Psycho-Analysis*, which may be taken as a typical example of an obsessional neurosis, in which the symptomatic acts of the sufferer bear a clear relation to the past occurrence which was the immediate cause of the outbreak of the disease.

A lady of nearly thirty years of age suffered from very severe obsessional symptoms . . . In the course of a day she would perform the following peculiar obsessive act, among others, several times over. She would run out of her room into an adjoining one, there take up a certain position at the table in the centre of the room, ring for her maid, give her a trivial order or send her away without, and then run back again. . . . Every time I had asked the patient, "Why do you do this? What is the meaning of it?" she had answered, "I don't know." But one day, after I had succeeded in overcoming a great hesitation on her part, involving a matter of principle, she suddenly did know, for she related the history of the obsessive act. More than ten years previously she had married a man much older than herself, who had proved impotent on the wedding night. Innumerable times on that night he had run out of his room into hers in order to make the attempt, but had failed every time. In the morning he had said angrily, "It's enough to disgrace one in the eyes of the maid who does the beds," and seizing a bottle of red ink which happened to be at hand, he poured it on the sheet, but not exactly in the place where such a mark might have been.

In interpreting the obsessive act of this patient Freud points out that she had identified herself with her husband, and acted his part in running from one room into another. Moreover, the table by which she stood symbolized the bed, a symbolism reinforced by the fact that the table covering had a stain on it, corresponding to the ink mark on the sheet. The act appears to be a repetition of the scene on the wedding night; but in fact it goes further.

> The kernel of it evidently lies in the calling of the maid, to whom she displays the mark, in contrast to her husband's words: "It's enough to disgrace one before the servant." In this way he, whose part she is playing, is *not* ashamed before the servant, the stain is where it ought to be. We see, therefore, that she has not simply repeated the scene, she has continued it and corrected it, transformed it into what it ought to have been. This implies something else, too, a correction of the circumstances which made that night so distressing, and which made the red ink necessary: namely, the husband's impotence. The obsessive act thus says: "No, it is not true, he was not disgraced before the servant, he was not impotent!" As in a dream she represents this wish as fulfilled, in a current obsessive act, which serves the purpose of restoring her husband's credit after that unfortunate incident.[1]

From this account of a typical obsessive act certain points may be noticed which will be of importance in our study of the development of religion. These I shall here state quite briefly and dogmatically without attempting to justify them. Their justification can be found in the pages of Freud's work from which the illustration is taken, so that it is perhaps unnecessary to enter into such details here. The points to be noticed are these:

(i) The obsessive acts—the ritual of the patient—reflects his or her unconscious wishes both positively and negatively: that is, they serve as expressions of, and as defences against, them.

[1] Freud: *Introductory Lects.*, etc., pp. 221–3.

(ii) The obsession begins by a fixation upon some event in the past. "In every one of our patients we learn by analysis that the symptoms and their effects have set the sufferer back into some past period of his life. In the majority of cases it is actually a very early phase of the life history which has been thus selected." [1]

(iii) The meaning of the obsessive act is in every case unknown to the sufferer; and the symptoms can be shown by an analysis to have been derived from mental processes which before treatment were unconscious. From this two things follow: (*a*) that the obsessive act is only to be understood if the unconscious motive behind it is brought to light, and (*b*) conversely, that without such an unconscious motive no symptom can arise: if the unconscious process is brought into consciousness the symptoms disappear.

(iv) The symptom—the obsessive act or ritual—is a repetition of, and a substitute for, something which has remained unconscious.

(v) In analysis the physician discovers memory-gaps or amnesias on the part of the patient. The symptoms of the neurosis are not connected by the patient with the event which caused them.

4. *The Interpretation of Totemism: Relations of Totemism and the Œdipus Complex*

We are now perhaps sufficiently equipped to turn our attention to the subject which really interests us—the phenomenon of religion in what appears to be its first form, Totemism. Indeed, our armoury has been rather hastily furnished, but if events prove that we are lacking in equipment, then we shall have to provide them as occasion demands. Accepting the Freudian view of the analogy between religion and the obsessional neurosis, we must now endeavour to discover the meaning of the "symptoms" of Totemism. We have already had occasion to mention the theriomorphic conception of God held by primitive man, which is at the base of

[1] Ibid., p. 232.

totemism and which largely conditions the form taken by totemistic worship. It is only necessary here to add this warning: that, having a fuller conception of God than even pre-Christian man (or, at least, a different conception), we must beware of speaking of a God of totemism, since the word "god" carries much more meaning for us than was associated by primitive man with the object of his worship. If, however, we bear this fact in mind, we may use the word "god" as a convenient term for the worshipped object, while remaining aware of how much more it means to us than it would have done to our remote ancestors.

The religious belief underlying Totemism is revealed in two ways—in its ceremonies and in its taboos; or, in other words, in its ritual and in its moral commands. Both of these appear to have had the character of obsessions: the worshipper, if we may so call him, felt the observance of them to have a compelling force upon him which he was powerless to resist—a compulsion which has remained as one of the characteristics of religion ever since, even though the beliefs and the forms of the ceremonial have undergone considerable modification or development. Moreover, both the rites and the prohibitions of Totemism must in accordance with the analogy of the obsessional neurosis, be regarded as symptomatic, since they both possess this same obsessive character. In fact they are to be regarded together and as depending upon one another, but for the sake of convenience they will have to be dealt with separately.

The most striking feature of Totemism appears to be its sacrificial ritual which consists of two parts, the killing of the totem-animal and the eating of its flesh by the members of the tribe. We need not concern ourselves in this study with the meaning which the totemist himself gives to such a ceremony, since, as has been shown by Theodor Reik in his book *Ritual*, and by others, the real meaning of a primitive ceremony or custom is almost invariably concealed from those who practice it, while the meaning they themselves attribute to it is nothing more than a rationalistic interpretation constructed by themselves. Indeed, if such beliefs and practices are to be understood on the model of the obsessional neurosis of the individual, the real motive or meaning must necessarily be hidden from them, simply because it is unconscious and therefore unknown.

If we treat these acts of killing and eating the totem-animal as if they were the symptoms of an obsessional neurosis, we shall expect to find in them the same features which were noticed above.[1] As has already been mentioned, the real meaning of Totemistic sacrifice, like many other primitive customs and beliefs, is unknown to the worshipper. This fact has caused much difficulty in the interpretation of savage ritual—a difficulty which only a method like that of Psycho-analysis can possibly hope to overcome. For when we say that the meaning of a particular rite or belief is unknown, we do not mean that its true interpretation and significance are non-existent, but rather that they exist unconsciously instead of consciously, or, if we like, that they have been forgotten. Such an ignorance of the true meaning of the rites of Totemism is seen to correspond with the memory-gaps or amnesias of neurotic patients which are brought to light during the course of analysis.

Further, the obsessive acts of killing and eating the totem-animal may be traced back to an event in the remote past which has been subsequently repressed and forgotten— namely, I would suggest, the sexual-aggressive act of Adam against God. These obsessive acts are, moreover, symbolic substitutes, as in a dream, for the fulfilment of desires which remain unconscious in the mind of the worshipper, and they reflect these unconscious wishes both positively and negatively.

Stated briefly in this way, such a theory must sound rather fantastic, but if it is examined more thoroughly it will per-haps sound more reasonable, as its various parts are seen to fit together. To see it all in its true perspective we must for a moment return to the theory put forward in the last chapter on the nature of Adam's sin. There it was suggested that man's first disobedience consisted in an act of the will,

[1] See pp. 96-7.

in the wish to claim independence from, and equality with, the Creator. Such a proud desire on the part of man, claiming the complete mastery of his own soul, could not by the very nature of God gain a real fulfilment, but only an imagined one, a mere fantasy. It must therefore have remained as a wish, which as a result of the repression (forgetting) of the knowledge of God lost its force, and so also became repressed or forgotten as its purpose, the abolition of man's rival, God, seemed to have been achieved. Or, looking at it in another way, the desire of man against God was repressed as are the incestuous desires of sons towards their mothers, which exist in infancy but are completely forgotten by the adult and which only reappear as a result of some abnormal development or experience. In fact then the desire for equality with God remained with the repressed knowledge of God at an unconscious level in the human mind, only to be reawakened later in human history. Here is not the place to discuss what the event may have been which caused this reawakening: it is sufficient for the present to suggest that some such experience must have occurred to cause it, but the nature of that experience will be dealt with at a later stage.

In attempting to reconstruct and interpret the outbreak of the universal obsessional neurosis, we have not yet dealt with the question why man chose an animal as part of his religious apparatus, if we may call it such; and this is perhaps as convenient a place as any to speak about it, before we come to the interpretation of the actual ceremonial. The origin of totemistic symbolism has been explained in various ways by different authors. Many of these explanations are, however, unsatisfactory, since they depend upon ideas, said to exist in the savage mind, of a certain affinity between mankind and the animals. If such ideas are not in fact the result rather than the cause of totemistic symbolism, then the argument is only put a stage further back, and a new question presents itself, namely, why the savage should feel any such affinity towards animals. It is true that certain animals display characteristics which may be admired or feared by humans, but this cannot be said of all of the animals which are found as totems. If the savage, in fact, feels such an affinity towards the animals, it is, I think, quite as reasonable to suggest that this is an artificially created feeling, springing from Totemism, as it is to say that an already existing sense of kinship with the animal world provided the pattern for Totemism. Later savages perhaps felt a common kinship with a particular animal because it was their totem, and from that the feeling of affinity with animals in general gradually grew up as a logical extension. A suggestion put forward by Freud[1] gives a clue to what may be a more reasonable explanation of the choice (if we may thus speak of an unconscious process) of an animal as the totem by primitive man. An analogy may be found in the study of dreams: as has already been explained above, one may distinguish between the manifest dream-content, that which is presented to the dreamer, and the true meaning of the dream, or its latent content. In order to make the dream acceptable to the psychic censorship the true content of the dream undergoes a process of distortion and symbolization, called by Freud the dream work, as a result of which the dreamer perceives not the real meaning of the dream but only an apparently meaningless sequence of what are in fact symbols. But the material, which goes to make up these symbols, does not arise in the mind in any haphazard manner. Freud[2] has classified the material and sources of dreams, and of this dream-material two classes— namely, recent and indifferent impressions of waking life, and forgotten impressions of childhood—need to be noticed here. As undoubtedly in primitive society animals would both provide vivid impressions during the period of infantile amnesia, and figure largely in the experiences of everyday life, they would also provide a large proportion of the dream material, and so appear in the dreams of primitive men more often perhaps than in those of their civilized descendants. If the analogy which has been suggested here is indeed a valid one, then it may be that the unconscious choice of an animal as the totem-god was governed by a similar distortion and sym-

---

[1] *Moses and Monotheism*, p. 133.
[2] *Interp. of Dreams*, Chapter V.

bolization. The knowledge of God, which was repressed in the unconscious, in its partial return to consciousness underwent a process of symbolization similar to that of the dreamwork and similar to that which may be discerned in the formation of symptoms by a neurotic individual. And further the form which that symbolization took was governed by similar principles, and thus the "god" of primitive man appeared in his dreams as an animal, since he accepted the symbol not for what it really was, but at its face value. Indeed, the form of the worshipped object may actually have been taken straight from the dreams of primitive man, as has been suggested by Lucretius, though it should be noted that he represents a later stage of religious development than the theriomorphic conceptions of primitive man.[1]

Now, if the totem animal is thus a symbolization of, and a substitute for, God, we may be able to understand more readily the meaning of the ritual and the prohibitions of Totemism, and we may offer the following explanation of its mysteries. If we regard the killing of the totem animal as if it were a symptom of an obsessional neurosis, it may not be too far-fetched to suggest that it represents the fulfilment of man's unconscious desire for supremacy over God in a symbolic form. Indeed, the killing of a rival is the surest and most permanent way of gaining an ascendancy over him. Thus, in the symbolic killing of the totem-animal man achieved the fulfilment of his unconscious wish: God was dead, and man could take his place: man had overcome God, and now reigned alone in creation. Man's wish was thus fulfilled in the obsessive act, in a manner similar to that in which unconscious desires find fulfilment in dreams.[2] This,

[1] See *De Rerum Natura*, V, 1169 ff.:

> Quippe etenim iam tum divum mortalia saecla
> egregias animo facies vigilante videbant
> et magis in somnis mirando corporis auctu.
> Hig igitur sensum tribuebant propterea quod
> membra movere videbantur vocesque superbas
> mittere pro facie praeclara et viribus amplis.

[2] Compare Freud: *Introductory Lects., etc.*, pp. 170-4, and p. 223.

however, is only one part of a more complex whole. As is the case in a neurosis, one such act once performed was not sufficient. This conquest of God was not complete and final: it had to be repeated, and repeated again. The relief was only temporary and did not serve to allay the sense of guilt which was partially reawakened by the killing of the totem, and was thus still as real as the unconscious desire which prompted that killing.[1] It was as a form of defence against this sense of guilt that the crime of killing the totem was shared amongst all the members of the tribe: all were equally guilty of its blood, and so none was wholly guilty as an individual. With the same object in view the peculiar taboos of totemism arose in order to prevent the individual from committing the communal crime. According to such an interpretation the killing of the totem is seen to be a positive expression of man's unconscious wishes. But by another interpretation, which is to be regarded rather as complementary rather than as alternative to this one, the killing of the totem appears as a negative expression—a denial—of those wishes. For, besides being a substitute-equivalent for God, the totem animal is also conceived to be in some way the representative of the tribe, whose members are blood-brothers of the totem,[2] a fact which may well have made the subsequent substitution

[1] What we may thus call the inefficacy of such compulsive acts in restoring complete harmony to man's soul is also a characteristic of later religion which it may be convenient to notice here. Thus, contrasting the sacrifice of the old Covenant with the sacrifice of Christ, the author of the Epistle to the Hebrews writes, "For the law having a shadow of good things to come, and not the very image of the things, can never with those sacrifices which they offered year by year continually make the comer thereunto perfect. For then would they not have ceased to be offered? because that the worshippers once purged should have had no more conscience of sins" (Hebrews, x, 1–2). So also the same writer speaks of the "weakness and unprofitableness" of the law, which can of itself make nothing perfect (compare Hebrews, vii, 18–19).

[2] See Robertson Smith: *Religion of the Semites*, p. 124: "In the totem stage of society each kinship or stock of savages believes itself to be physically akin to some natural kind of animate or inanimate things, most generally to some kind of animal. Every animal of this kind is looked upon as a brother."

of a human victim possible. This being so, in killing the totem animal primitive man was also acting the part of God (as the lady in the example acted the part of her husband) and thus was also, in a manner, killing himself—that is, more explicitly, he was inflicting upon himself through his representative the punishment for his unconscious desires that such impious thoughts demanded. In such a way the symbolic fulfilment of his desires against God is at the same time its own symbolic punishment.

If the murder of the totem is a positive fulfilment of the unconscious desire to murder God, it is perhaps more easy to understand the meaning of the eating of the totem animal when it had been killed.[1] By partaking of the flesh and blood of the dead god, the life and strength of the god is appropriated by the eater, thus fulfilling another part of man's unconscious (repressed) desire—the desire for immortality, which is perhaps the most coveted attribute of the Creator. The immortal nature of the eternal God is symbolically incorporated into the life of man: the divine flesh is consumed by the human, and thus humanity itself becomes divine and immortal.

Before proceeding to examine the meaning of the two primary taboos, which must also be classed as obsessions like the symbolic acts already mentioned, it may be convenient to ask at this point why it was that the "religious neurosis" of primitive man took the particular form that it did. If this question can be answered satisfactorily, then two other difficulties will also be resolved—namely, (i) why non-theistic science has traced the origin of religion back to the alleged murder of the human father of the primeval horde, and (ii) why it was that the taboo forbidding incest arose. This question will be answered more simply if we return for a moment to consider the theory put forward by Freud in *Moses and Monotheism* to account for the appearance of

[1] Here we may note that according to the interpretation given here the killing of the totem is more than a merely necessary prelude to its consumption; but on the other hand the eating of the totem may be regarded as a logical corollary of its death.

Christianity. According to the suggestions he there makes, it would appear that the traumatic experience in the infancy of the human race was the first murder of the father: but that a full realization of the neurosis only occurred after something which may also perhaps be termed traumatic—namely, the murder of Jesus Christ. In other words, it is argued that the immediate cause of the religion of Paul was the death of Jesus, but that its ultimate cause was to be traced back to the remote prehistory of mankind. Moreover, if we look at any case of a neurosis in an individual, we cannot help noticing that what are defined as traumatic experiences, (e.g. a railway accident, or the unfortunate occurrences on the wedding night in the example quoted earlier), only prove to be "traumatic", and thus the cause of neurosis, when they do actually result in the outbreak of neurotic symptoms. Looked at it another way, what is meant by this is that a particular experience may occur to two different persons: in every respect the experience may be the same for both of them, but in the one it may bring on the outbreak of a neurosis, while in the other it may not. In other words, every shocking experience does not bring on a neurosis. Too great a pre-occupation with the causation and formation of neurosis may easily blind us to this simple fact, but when once it is noticed we are forced to the conclusion that the one person who suffered such a shock would probably have developed neurotic symptoms anyway at some time or another, while the other would not have done so. The real root and ultimate cause of the trouble appears therefore to lie far behind and beneath the immediate and apparent cause. If we consider once again the example quoted from Freud, we may recall that our first reaction may well have been to say, "How stupid: there must have been something wrong with her already." The events on the wedding night thus appear as the immediate cause of the neurotic outbreak, and they also condition the form which is taken by the symptoms.[1]

Now if we are not mistaken in thus supposing an immediate and an ultimate cause behind the actual outbreak of a

[1] Compare Freud: *Introductory Lects.*, etc., pp. 231–2.

neurosis, then this distinction may help us to understand more about the origin of Totemism. It would seem that before a neurosis can break out some experience must occur, or may be assumed to have occurred, which may be called the immediate cause of the outbreak. In answer, therefore, to the questions, what was the immediate cause of the origin of Totemism and what conditioned the form taken by Totemism (we have already traced its ultimate cause to the sin of Adam against God), I am going to suggest that we are to look for it in that act in the now remote past when the sons banded together and slew their father, in the murder of the father of the primeval horde about which we have already heard so much.[1] If this suggestion is correct then three things follow: (i) the connection between the taboo against incest and the sin of Adam against God can be more readily seen; (ii) the murder of the father of the primal horde falls into its proper place in the general scheme of human history; and (iii) the sense of guilt belonging to that murder (and subsequently to the incestuous desires of the Œdipus complex type) is seen to be really derived from the unconscious sense of guilt arising from Adam's sin, as has already been suggested on other grounds with regard to sexuality in general. Further it may be suggested, according to this view, that the hatred of the father which constitutes one part of the Œdipus complex is a projection of man's unconscious hostile feelings towards God.

[1] This is one possible line of argument, which assumes the general truth of the Freudian view of man's prehistory. As I have already pointed out, I have accepted this view for the sake of argument, in accordance with the principle that nothing should be rejected of the Freudian system except such theories as were not based on Psychoanalytic investigation, or such as sprang from the presupposition that God is non-existent. As Freud's view of primitive man's social organization seems to rest on psychological grounds, it seemed to be necessary to find for it a place in this tentative reconstruction of the origin of religion. If, however, Freud's theory on this subject is incorrect, then I would make two suggestions which are presented as possible alternatives: (1) that some other event, which caused the outbreak of the religious neurosis, may have to be assumed; or (2) that the outbreak occurred spontaneously after a period of latency, as is the case in certain cases of neurosis in individuals.

These internal feelings are externalized; they are treated as though they were acting not from within but from without. The human father thus becomes, as it were, a type of God, or, if we like, a God-substitute; and, indeed, such a transference of feeling from the divine creator to the human father is not so difficult to understand when we consider the fact that the human father stands in an almost identical relation to the individual as God does to the race.[1] This is no doubt the reason why the Œdipus complex possesses such a great energy-charge (cathexis) in the individual.

If then we are to see in the murder of the father of the primitive horde the immediate cause of the return of the repressed desires of man against God and of the repressed sense of guilt in the form of obsessive symptoms, as well as the force determining the form of those symptoms, we shall also be able to see how the taboos against incest and against killing the totem-animal fit into their places in a religious view of man's history. Both are identical in intention: both represent the unconscious wishes of the race negatively; that is to say, they are defences against those wishes, and seek to preserve the individual from giving expression to them and so from repeating the primal sin of mankind. Thus the meaning of the prohibition against the murder of the totem-animal, which is the substitute for God, is to be explained primarily as a protection for the individual from falling into the sin of attempting to gain superiority over God by killing the God-symbol, and perhaps secondarily as a protection for him from assuming the role of God in killing the totem-animal in its part of a mankind-substitute. Further, if we are

---

[1] We may be reminded in this connection of Saint Paul's words in Ephesians, iii, 15, τούτου χάριν κάμπτω τὰ γόνατά μου πρὸς τὸν πατέρα, ἐξ οὗ πᾶσα πατριὰ ἐν οὐρανοῖς καὶ ἐπὶ γῆς ὀνομάζεται, particularly when we observe the connection between πατήρ and πατριά —a connection obscured in the English Version's translation "family" for the latter, though the R.V. margin has "Gk.—fatherhood". It is also significant that this connection between the human father and God is particularly noticed by Freud, who, because he bases his theory on the presupposition that God does not exist, comes to the conclusion that God is merely a father-substitute.

to see in the idea of the relations of a man to his father a projection of mankind's relations towards God, then the real meaning of the taboo forbidding incest may also be understood on similar lines. In a few words, the sin of incest lies not so much in the affection shown towards the mother, which is essentially a natural and necessary relationship, but in the hostility towards the father. Here again, we may notice what we observed earlier in the relation of sexual and aggressive impulses—the phenomenon of the displacement of moral values. In condemning incest the moral emphasis is directed on to the tender (sexual) relationship to the mother, rather than the hostile (aggressive) relationship to the father. Incest, however, is in fact another way in which the father may be overcome and dispossessed; and if we are right in supposing that in this connection also the father is to be regarded as a God-substitute, then, like the taboo against murder, this taboo forbidding incest is also a protection for the individual from attempting to take for himself the place of God.[1] Such a view may also explain why incestuous marriage (e.g., between brother and sister) was not merely permitted but actually enjoined upon certain rulers who were regarded as being themselves divine. If they were themselves gods the displacement of the human father would not have the same symbolic meaning for them as for ordinary mortals. Thus the two chief taboos are seen to be negative (i.e., defensive) expressions of man's unconscious desires towards God— desires which also find expression, both positive and negative, in the ritual killing and eating of the totem-animal.

Such a theory as has been set out here may also serve to relate other features of totemism to a theistic philosophy of

[1] It is perhaps not unreasonable to suppose that the first prohibition of incest was limited to a prohibition of sexual relations between the son and his mother, and that this was subsequently broadened in its scope to include other "incestuous" relationships. Such a process is not difficult to explain. If the real meaning of the incest-taboo remained, like that of obsessive symptoms generally, at an unconscious level, then this process of widening its original scope appears to be a conscious rationalization of the prohibition, so that the marriage of all close relations was forbidden.

life. In his book *Ritual*, Theodor Reik endeavours to prove, on Psycho-analytic grounds, that the puberty-rites of savages are an unconscious attempt to break what may be called the spell of the Œdipus complex, and to restore the relationship of the son to the father by a process of spiritual rebirth in a ceremony which includes the rite of circumcision. This is not the place to repeat or discuss at length the arguments by which he supports this theory. All we need to say is, that if the Psycho-analytic method is a valid one, and if it is applied correctly, then we shall accept this theory in so far as it does not depend on any absolute presupposition. For our present purpose, therefore, it will be sufficient to make the suggestion that, if we are not mistaken in supposing that the hostility of the son towards the father is in fact a projection of man's hostility towards God, then the real intention of such puberty rites is the restoration of the relationship of man, not so much with his father, as with God, and as such is on a par with the taboos against murder and incest. So too, if, as is suggested by Freud, circumcision is a symbolic substitute for castration,[1] the administration of that rite at the time of the puberty rebirth ceremonies may also signify in a symbolic manner man's repudiation of his unconscious wishes against God and his submission to the God-substitute, that is, his father. It may also be suggested that the rite of circumcision, if it is a substitute for castration, is to be regarded as a manifestation of an unconscious desire for punishment which forms part of every obsessional neurosis.[2] If this is so then this need for punishment, felt unconsciously by man, must appear as a product of his repressed sense of guilt, and perhaps explains why circumcision remained such an indelible feature of religion, even when the other rites and ceremonies of Totemism had been so transformed as to be

[1] "I think that there can be no doubt that circumcision, a practice common to so many peoples, is an equivalent and replacement of castration"—*Introductory Lects., etc.*, p. 139.

[2] Thus Freud writes: "It seems as though this factor, the unconscious need for punishment, plays a part in every neurotic disease"—*New Introductory Lects., etc.*, p. 140.

almost unrecognizable, as for example among the Jews. Though it is perhaps out of its logical place here, we should notice in this connection the symbolic use of circumcision made in the Old Testament and by Saint Paul.[1] To this unconscious desire for punishment, in itself a manifestation of the sense of guilt, and so too a negative expression of man's desires against God, may also be attributed other forms of self-denial and self-effacement in religion, such as fasting and asceticism in general.

It is also possible to give another interpretation of the rite of circumcision complementary to those given immediately above, according to which we may see in it a positive expression of man's unconscious desires, as well as an expression of the negative desire for punishment. In many strands of the primitive myth of the origin of death, the coveted gift of immortality is gained by the serpent, or by some other animal, which is supposed to renew its youth perpetually by casting its skin—a process which, according to some versions, was also the method by which the first human beings renewed their youth.[2]   When speaking earlier of these Fall myths, we had occasion to suggest that in some way or another they had a sexually symbolic significance. What I would now go on to suggest is that not only may the apple in the Adam and Eve story be a sexual symbol, but that this may also be true of the serpent, which in dreams is reckoned, like many other animals, to be a symbol of the penis.[3] Now if, in the minds

[1] Compare Deuteronomy, x, 16: "Circumcise therefore the foreskins of your heart"; Jeremiah, iv, 4: "Circumcise yourselves to the Lord, and take away the foreskins of your heart, ye men of Judah, and inhabitants of Jerusalem"; and Romans, ii, 28–9: "For he is not a Jew, which is one outwardly in the flesh: but he is a Jew, which is one inwardly; and circumcision is that of the heart, in the spirit and not in the letter."

[2] See Frazer: *Folk-Lore in the Old Testament* (Abridged Edition), pp. 26 ff.

[3] See Freud: *Interp. of Dreams*, p. 339; *Introductory Lects., etc.,* p. 130. In this connection it is of interest to notice the association of serpents, or their human counterparts, with the primitive rites of sexual initiation: see Pierre Gordon: *L'Initiation Sexuelle et l'Evolution Religieuse*, Presses Universitaires de France, 1946, pp. 24 and 29 f.

of primitive men the serpent is immortal because it sheds its skin, and if to them also the serpent is a phallic symbol, we may perhaps arrive at this interpretation of the rite of circumcision. As the removal of the skin from the serpent ensures the renewal of its youth, so the symbolic removal of the foreskin by circumcision is intended unconsciously to ensure the immortality of the person circumcised. If this is so, then the rite is a positive expression of man's unconscious desire for immortality, and, like the killing of the totem-animal is at once the fulfilment and the punishment of that desire. This last interpretation of the custom of circumcision is purely speculative, and is only put forward as such. There are, however, certain considerations which may make it appear more plausible than it may otherwise seem. If it is correct, then it may perhaps make more understandable the connection between the circumcision of Abraham and the promise of what amounts to immortality to him through his seed.[1] Further, this interpretation may supply the true unconscious motive for this custom, which by some savages is supposed to ensure the continuation of life after death.[2] Moreover, such an explanation of circumcision may help us, when we come to speak of the Christian Sacraments, to appreciate part of the significance of Baptism which in Christianity took the place of circumcision in Judaism.

This is perhaps a convenient point at which to pause for a moment in order to survey the ground we have covered before we again move forward. In brief, we have endeavoured

[1] See Genesis, xvii, 19–26. "And God said, Sarah thy wife shall bear thee a son indeed; and thou shalt call his name Isaac: and I will establish my covenant with him for an everlasting covenant, and with his seed after him. And as for Ishmael, I have heard thee; Behold, I have blessed him, and will make him fruitful, and will multiply him exceedingly; . . . And Abraham took Ishmael his son, and all that were born in his house, and all that were bought with his money, every male among the men of Abraham's house; and circumcised the flesh of their foreskin in the self-same day, as God had said unto him. And Abraham was ninety years old and nine, when he was circumcised in the flesh of his foreskin . . ."

[2] Compare S. A. Cook's note in Robertson Smith: *Religion of the Semites*, p. 609.

to show how the first religion of man, Totemism, may be interpreted on the model of an obsessional neurosis in an individual; how that religion consists of symptomatic ceremonies and prohibitions which express both positively and negatively the repressed wishes of man against God; and how the form taken by those ceremonies and prohibitions was conditioned by the social revolution which was the immediate cause for the appearance of the symptoms. There is, however, one objection in particular which may be raised against this interpretation of Totemism—namely, that the sexual character of the taboo forbidding incest and of the savage puberty rites make it difficult to see in them, and so too in the rest of Totemism, a partial return from the unconscious, in the form of symptoms, of repressed wishes against God, and of the sense of guilt consequent upon a sin against the Creator. In answer to this, two points may be taken into consideration. The form taken by the obsessional symptoms are not necessarily to be regarded as directly dependent on the ultimate cause of the neurosis, but rather as symbolic and as being conditioned in regard to the form of the symbols by the immediate cause of it.[1] A connection, however, is also to be seen which may have been forgotten. If we were correct in connecting the origin of sin in Adam with the exercise of the sexual function, as well as with the aggressive instinct of man, we may not be quite so surprised if we find an obsessional neurosis breaking out as an ultimate result of Adam's sexual-aggressive sin against God, and that that neurosis finds its symptomatic repression in obsessive acts and prohibitions, some of which are connected not only with the aggressive, but also with the sexual impulse of man. Thus the sexual-aggressive Œdipus complex is by its very nature inextricably entangled with what we may call the Adam complex—i.e., with the complex issuing from, or following the pattern of, the primal sin of man against God—and the former is seen almost inevitably to condition the form of the symptomatic

[1] Compare with this the examples and interpretations of obsessions and compulsions given by V. E. Fisher in his book, *An Introduction to Abnormal Psychology*, pp. 213–24.

expressions of the latter. Moreover, apart from any considerations such as these, it would be foolish to underestimate the impact which the great mysteries of both individual and mass life, the inescapable mysteries of sexuality and death, must have made on the minds of our primitive ancestors, and it would therefore be the more surprising if these mysteries were not reflected in their religion.

5. *The Development of Religion: Revelation as the Return of the Repressed*

We may now move forward again, and here the road is well-trodden and our steps can be more rapid. It is hardly necessary here to trace in detail the development of religion from primitive Totemism to the more familiar forms of heathen and Jewish worship. If we are willing to accept the analogy between the symptoms of an obsessional neurosis and the ceremonies and observances of Totemism, and therefore also to accept the unconscious basis of Totemism, then it is perhaps easier to understand the processes which made the development of religion possible—namely, the change from the theriomorphic to the anthropomorphic conception of God; the development from the quasi-sacramental sacrifices of Totemism to the sin-offerings and burnt offerings and the whole sacrificial system of post-exilic Judaism; and the growth of social and moral law, as a result of the broadening of the scope of the Taboos against incest and the killing of the totem-animal so that they emerged as the commandments forbidding adultery and murder.

These changes in pre-Christian religion are sometimes attributed to the growing intelligence of humanity, and to a process of rationalizing by man of what appeared illogical and unnatural to his developing mental faculties. Such an explanation, however, is not sufficient, for it does not go deep enough: the enquirer is no nearer to an understanding of the real meaning or motive of the changes. We must, therefore, examine this explanation, and see if it is possible from it to approach nearer to a more positive explanation. We are confronted by a question which falls into three parts: why did man's conception of God, of sacrifice, and of morality, change; or perhaps we should speak of his conception of those things later known as God, sacrifice, and morality. Here we are presented with the three different aspects of the same question, and the Theologian, as well as the Scientist, has his solution of the problem to offer; he will probably suggest that the change came about as a result of divine revelation, by which we are to understand that God reveals certain items of information to particular chosen individuals, or directs their thought into channels different from those of other people not similarly inspired. The theory of Revelation, however, seems to suffer from a defect similar to that of the theory of Rationalization. They both attempt to set the process of religious development in a logical order, but in order to bring this about supply what may appear to their opponents to be an indefinite and extra-human something as the cause of the process; in other words, neither theory supplies a sufficient or universally acceptable operative force or motive for the process to take place.

By this I mean that neither theory really furnishes an adequate explanation of itself. If the development of religion is ascribed to divine revelation, we are not told why man was willing to receive, or able to recognize, that revelation, nor how it was assimilated by him. If we are told that man received this divine inspiration through dreams or angelic visitations, then we may quite justifiably be tempted to ask, by what sure and certain guide did they interpret their dreams, or who were the angels who spoke to them: how, in other words, can we test this revelation. We may recall in this connection that to say "God spoke to me in a dream" is really no more than saying "I dreamed that God spoke to me". If it is said that the "inspired" persons simply *thought* such-and-such about God, then the inspiration ceases to be divine, and the revelation becomes merely human conjecture which happens to coincide with our own opinions or beliefs. Similarly, if the process of development is ascribed to rationalization on the part of man of his primitive theories

120

and beliefs, that is, to the growing awareness of his difference from the animals and to the development of his ideas regarding personal property and social convenience, then we are still not informed why man should undergo such a process of development, and why he should not have remained, like Peter Pan, an intellectual infant. To attribute man's religious development to an evolutionary process, as if progress were an inevitable law of nature, is merely to describe that development in different terms; it still does not tell us why it all happened.

In spite of their different approach to the subject, however, both these theories appear to share in the view that the primary and decisive change was in man's conception of God, and that his changed conception of worship and morality was secondary, inasmuch as it was conditioned by his ideas about God. Our present problem, therefore, may be said to be to explain the development of religion in terms which take into account and explain the ideas of both Revelation and Rationalization. If, however, we take into consideration what has been said earlier, it may not be so difficult to effect a synthesis between these apparently mutually exclusive ideas. An indication has already been given, and it only remains now to justify and expand a suggestion made in the first chapter of this study: and this justification will depend primarily upon belief in the existence of God as the ultimate source of what is "revealed", and secondarily upon the acceptance of the theory of an unconscious system the content of which may be transmitted from one generation to another. If then we also accept the view put forward earlier that, as a result of Adam's sin, the knowledge of God which he possessed consciously was not abolished, but repressed by man, we are presented with a fact which may be used to throw light on the problem of the development of religion.

The immediate problem of reconciling the ideas of Revelation and Rationalization really arises because both are explanations of the same process in different terms and from different points of view. Indeed it seems inevitable that, if we subject any process to minute examination from a particular standpoint, we shall see more clearly some parts of it, while others will be more obscured, than if we had conducted our examination from some other position. We may perhaps compare this with the two different aspects presented by the same countryside when it is viewed from two different places: or, if further illustration is needed, we may easily imagine how unrecognizably different the heavens would appear, could the observer be transported from the earth to the vicinity of one of the more distant stars. I would, therefore, suggest, that it is due to a kind of intellectual parallax, if we may use the phrase, that the ideas of Rationalization and Revelation appear to be incompatible. Now, if we are right in supposing that before Adam's sin man knew God face to face, as we say "man to man", then it is not, I think, unreasonable also to suppose that the processes either of Revelation (i.e., direct action by God upon the human mind), or of Rationalization (i.e., the idea of man's intellectual development), could not give to man a fuller knowledge of God than he had before he had sinned. In other words, if a complete knowledge of God was contained in a repressed state in man's unconscious, then that knowledge was as complete and full as any which could be given to man from outside, by Revelation, or which man could deduce for himself by conscious logical processes, by Rationalization. If then the knowledge already possessed unconsciously is imagined to be brought back to consciousness, the ideas which we have been discussing become unnecessary hypotheses, and their imperfections may be more easily understood. We shall be able to view our imaginary landscape not from the North only or from the South, but from above, and see it in an entirety which the other points of view do not permit.

But, it may be argued, is such a view possible, and if it is, is it really compatible with belief in God, in particular with belief in the idea of the Holy Spirit "who spake by the prophets"? If we are correct in assuming that the knowledge of God was repressed as a result of the Fall, then we must also acknowledge that that knowledge continued to exist in the unconscious. According to the psycho-analytic theory of the unconscious such repressed material is not abolished or extinguished by the process of repression, but it persists at an unconscious level and may, still at that level, be transmitted to subsequent generations. Moreover, under certain circumstances, this repressed material may return partially into consciousness. This whole process has been described, and, if we are to accept the validity of the Psycho-analytic method, psychologically justified by Freud in his works, from one of which we may quote the following:

> The forgotten material is not extinguished, only "repressed"; its traces are extant in the memory in this original freshness, but they are isolated by "counter-cathexes". They cannot establish contact with the other intellectual processes; they are unconscious, inaccessible to consciousness . . .
>
> This repressed material retains its impetus to penetrate into consciousness. It reaches its aim when three conditions are present. (i) When the strength of counter-cathexis is diminished by an illness which acts on the Ego itself, or through a different distribution of cathexis in the Ego as happens regularly during sleep. (ii) When those instincts attached to the repressed material become strengthened. The processes during puberty provide the best example of this. (iii) Whenever recent events produce impressions or experiences which are so much like the repressed material that they have the power to awaken it. Thus the recent material gets strengthened by the latent energy of the repressed, and the repressed material produces its effect behind the recent material and with its help . . . In none of the three cases does the material that had been repressed succeed in reaching consciousness unimpeded or without change. It must always undergo distortions which bear witness to the not entirely overcome resistance derived from the counter-cathexis, or else to the modifying influence of a recent experience or to both.[1]

Before we can apply this theory to the subject of Revelation as a return of the repressed knowledge of God, we must be certain that the three necessary conditions for such a return, as laid down by Freud, are in fact present. As we have hitherto accepted the analogy between the origin of religion

[1] *Moses and Monotheism*, pp. 152–3.

and the outbreak of a neurosis as valid, then we may see the first condition satisfied by the "religious neurosis" of Totemism, which resulted from the murder of the father of the primeval horde; through this act too the second and third conditions are also satisfied, the former by the strengthening of the sexual and aggressive impulses which prompted the deed, and the latter by the apparent similarity between the sexual-aggressive crime against the human father and the sin of Adam against God. The possibility of such a return of repressed material has already been used by Freud to explain the origin of Totemism and the development of religion after the time of Moses; and it is also in accordance with this analogy with the individual neurosis that we have tried to trace the beginnings of religion, though from a different presupposition from that which has been assumed to be the basis of the Freudian reconstruction. Making allowance, therefore, for this difference of presupposition—that is, by assuming God rather than the Father of the primeval horde as the object of the repressed thoughts—I would suggest that, as regards the method and operative force—the how and why— by which the development of the idea of God came about, the Freudian theory of the return of repressed material provides a solution of the problem nearer to the truth than we can perhaps otherwise approach. In other words, what we perceive as if it were revelation may, in fact, be nothing else than the re-emergence from the unconscious of the repressed knowledge of God and the repressed sense of guilt. If such a view is not mistaken, then the gradualness and incompleteness of such "revelation", as well as the contradictions between the revelations vouchsafed to different persons, are seen to be due to the imperfection and distortion attending the return of the repressed material to consciousness, and to the differing personal circumstances of each individual prophet or seer. The theory of Revelation by God to chosen individuals may therefore be regarded as the simplest, although an inadequate explanation of the phenomenon of a developing idea of God, that is, from the point of view of Religion: while the same may also be said of the scientific theory that religious development is to be understood in terms of the growing intellectual faculties of mankind.

As men, as a part of God's creation, we can only understand the process of divine-human intercourse from the human point of view. Thus when we speak of God's Forgiveness, we are speaking strictly not so much from experience of God forgiving but of being forgiven by God; we speak of God forgiving only by analogy to human experience which we already know. The same, indeed, applies to many of the terms by which religious experience is described. So too when we speak of Revelation we can only speak of it from the human end, and by analogy to previous human experience; we feel not so much that God is revealing something to us, as that we are acquiring some new knowledge from an apparently unknown source. What is thus spoken of as being revealed by God must, moreover, be recognized and appropriated by man; it can only be fully understood by man if it is in a sense a recognition of something which he really knew already, and I do not think it is a case of finding an unnecessarily complicated explanation of a simple process if we add that this seems to imply a previous knowledge of God buried in the unconscious and brought to consciousness by the appropriate stimulus. We may remark in passing that in principle this is no new theory; with it we may compare Plato's idea of ἀνάμνησις.[1] If therefore man in the beginning knew God face to face, it seems to be a reasonable hypothesis that the developing idea of the nature of God is a return of the repressed, a recollection of that knowledge of God which had been lost, inaccessible in the unconscious system of mankind. Nor does such a theory detract from the religious man's belief in the divine direction and control of human life; for it may as well have been the purpose of God that man should reacquire his knowledge of the Creator in this way, as that God should reveal himself by the direct inspiration of particular individuals. Since we are not in a position to read the divine mind, we cannot say that a

[1] Compare Ritter and Preller: *Historia Philosophiae Graecae* (10th Edn.), § 334, *c.*, p. 265.

particular theory of the development of religion is impossible because it does not conform with our own ideas or prejudices. All things remain in the hands of God, and the only true test of a theory is if it explains satisfactorily the observable phenomena.

The theory which I have endeavoured to put forward here may perhaps appear to be rather ambitious and too comprehensive in its scope to be thoroughly sound. Our first reaction to it will no doubt be to think that, even if we accept the premisses on which it is based, there must be a catch in it somewhere. I would, however, submit that novelty is not necessarily synonymous with inaccuracy. I trust that I may not appear high-minded if I point out that the theory that the earth and the other planets move in regular orbits round the sun, rather than that the sun and the planets move in epicycles round the earth, was at one time a novel theory which though it explained the facts more simply, was not at the time embraced without great suspicion. Moreover I would suggest that such a view of the development of religion not only explains adequately the general progress of religious thought on the nature of God, but it also accounts for what may be called the collateral developments of religion, among which may be included the ideas of the necessity for asceticism and sacrifice as integral parts of true religion.

The development of the ideas underlying sacrifice follow more or less logically and directly from the development of the idea of God. It is a fact sufficiently well attested elsewhere that ceremonial acts persist long after their original significance is forgotten, and that new meanings are attached to them. If, however, as has been suggested, the original meaning of sacrifice was unknown because it was unconscious, then it is more easy to see why a new meaning should be given to it, especially when the idea of God changed. When in process of time man had developed an anthropomorphic conception of the object of his worship, it is not surprising that he began to think of animal sacrifice as an offering to God rather than as a meal shared with him and as the killing of the God-substitute.[1] Apart from the change of meaning of such a development being a reasonable assumption in view of the development of the idea of God, we may also trace a reason for such a change taking place in the desire for punishment and self-abnegation which, as has already been pointed out, forms a part of every neurosis, and which, in the case of the Jews, was emphasized by their own political experiences. Further, if we are right in believing that the ultimate origin of religion is to be found in the repression of the sexual-aggressive desire of man against God, and that the emergence of religion resulted, on the pattern of the obsessional neurosis in the individual, from the sexual-aggressive act of the sons in killing the father as its immediate cause, then we may not find such difficulty in seeing why the sexual instinct received at one time a positive, and at others a negative, expression in religious beliefs and practices. Without going into any detailed examination of the practice of sexual indulgence which seems to form part of some manifestations of religion, I would merely suggest that they may be accounted for in this way, and are therefore as truly religious as other practices which are more in line with Christian thought. They may be regarded as similar in their unconscious motivation to the killing and eating of the totem-animal, in so far as that is a positive expression of man's aggressive desire against God. We are, however, on surer ground, when we look at such practices as fasting and sexual asceticism. It has already been pointed out that the taboo forbidding incest is a negative (defensive) expression of man's unconscious wishes; when therefore we take into account the developing idea of God and consequent upon that of the development of the rationale of sacrifice from the quasi-sacramental totem-feast to the piacular offering, we may not perhaps be mistaken in conjecturing that the taboo against incest lost its true (though unrealized) significance and came

[1] A parallel development from the sacred meal to the sacrificial offering may perhaps be seen in the changes which have brought the primitive Christian Eucharist of New Testament times to the Roman Mass of the present day.

to be looked on as a form of conscious self-denial and self-punishment, that is, quite apart from its original symbolic meaning as a repudiation of unconscious desires. If then the renunciation of the gratification of the desire for incest came to be regarded as a form of spiritual abstinence, it may well be that the idea of sexual renunciation in general, even within the permitted relationship of marriage, came to be regarded as pleasing to God.[1] Such a view of asceticism also conforms with what has been said regarding the development of sacrifice; like that it is as well a manifestation of a desire and need for punishment.

Brief though this survey of the development of religion may be, it will perhaps suffice to indicate the causes of that development, which may be traced ultimately to the unconscious origin of religion, and to the gradual and distorted return of repressed material to consciousness. Throughout it has been assumed that what we call primitive religion is analogous to the obsessive symptoms of an obsessional neurosis; and the development of religious practice and belief again find an analogy in the psychology of individuals not only in the actual return of the repressed but also in the changing forms of obsessive symptoms shown by some patients.[2] If such a view is, in fact, correct, as I believe it is, then we must be prepared to recognize religion as an unconscious and spontaneous attempt on the part of man to

[1] It may also be suggested that the Prophetic idea of sin against God being called fornication may have been in part conditioned by this view of sexual indulgence and self-denial. See Ezekiel, xvi, 15 ff.: "But thou didst trust in thine own beauty, and playedst the harlot because of thy renown, and pouredst out thy fornications on everyone that passed by . . . Thou hast also taken thy fair jewels of my gold and of my silver, which I have given thee, and madest to thyself images of men, and didst commit whoredom with them . . . thou hast also built unto thee an eminent place and hast made thee a high place in every street." Compare also 2 Chronicles, xxi, 11: "Moreover he made high places in the mountains of Judah, and caused the inhabitants of Jerusalem to commit fornication, and compelled Judah thereto."

[2] Compare the case quoted by Fisher: *An Introduction to Abnormal Psychology*, pp. 221 ff.

resolve the endopsychic conflict resulting from his sin against God—the conflict, that is, between his unconscious desires and his unconscious sense of guilt. Heathen religion thus achieves a result similar to that gained from an obsessional neurosis; it alleviates temporarily the mental disharmony, but it can give no permanent cure so long as, and because, the real cause of that disorder remains unconscious, or at most only imperfectly conscious. If, therefore, we are rightly to compare religion—and here, of course, we are speaking still of pre-Christian religion—with a mental disease, we may well ask if any "cure" is possible of such religious obsessions. The answer to this question is, I believe, to be found in the life and death of Jesus Christ and through faith in him as our Saviour; and here again we may see an analogy to the Psycho-analytic theory of the neurosis—but here the comparison is not with the symptoms of the disease but with its cure, with Psycho-analytic therapy.

It may appear to some to be unjustifiable to press the analogy between religion and the obsessional neurosis so far as this, but I would only point out that by accepting the analogy in the first place for the sake of argument, we are compelled to carry it on to the end, unless we would abandon the whole of our argument as far as it has gone. In other words, if we are not willing to see in Christianity the cure of the soul's disease, we shall have to accept the Freudian view that it is merely another form of that disease. It will therefore be the purpose of the last part of this essay to see if it is possible to translate the Christian experience of salvation through Jesus Christ into the terms of Psycho-analysis.

6. *The Psycho-analytic Therapy and Salvation*

For a complete account and explanation of the principles of Psycho-analytic therapy I must refer readers to works dealing with the clinical aspects of Psycho-analysis. Such a detailed account would be out of place here, and I shall therefore limit myself to what must be rather a cursory outline of the aim and method of Psycho-analysis. The first object of the Psycho-analyst is to find out and so bring to consciousness the repressed conflict of the patient, which causes his illness. This is accomplished by various means, in particular by dream interpretation, the association of ideas, and the interpretation of the obsessive symptoms. In the early days of Psycho-analysis hypnotism was also employed, but was later abandoned, and this abandonment of hypnosis marked the beginning of Psycho-analysis proper. At first it was believed that by thus pointing out to the patient the meaning of his obsessive symptoms a cure could be effected. Thus Freud says:

> What then have we to do in order to bring what is unconscious in the patient into consciousness? At one time we thought that would be very simple; all we need do would be to identify this unconscious matter and then tell the patient what it was. However, we know already that that was a shortsighted mistake. Our knowledge of what is unconscious in him is not equivalent to his knowledge of it; when we tell him what we know he does not assimilate it *in place of* his own unconscious thoughts, but *alongside* of them, and very little has been changed.[1]

Not only must the unconscious material be brought to consciousness, but the repression itself must be removed; and to achieve this the resistance which maintains the repression must be overcome, and this forms the second and distinctive phase of the Psycho-analytic work—namely, to search out and bring to light this resistance, which arose in the Ego to ensure the continued repression of the unwelcome thoughts. However, as this process is carried on a new and unexpected phenomenon manifests itself, what is called the Transference, which Freud defines as "a transference of feelings on to the person of the physician". To cut a long story short, Freud points out that this Transference is in fact a repetition of the feelings which the patient had in the remote past, and is a reproduction of his or her infantile emotions towards the parents, appearing, according to the sex of the physician, as either hostility or affection, which Psycho-analysis recognizes

[1] *Introductory Lects., etc.,* p. 364.

as ambivalent manifestations of the same emotion. In this way, as the result of the Transference, a kind of new temporary neurosis is set up in which the symptoms of the old neurosis are invested with a new meaning corresponding to the new relationship to the physician, and lose their original significance which corresponded to the old relationship to the parents. However, so far from being a hindrance to the cure, the Transference may be utilized to help forward its course, inasmuch as it establishes a condition of suggestibility on the part of the patient towards the physician. Moreover, it is only in mental disorders, such as hysteria and obsessional neurosis, in which this transference of the libido is possible that the sufferer is amenable to Psycho-analytic therapy. How this Transference actually works out in practice may be more clearly understood if we read what Freud himself has to say about it.

In order to dissolve the symptoms it is necessary to go back to the point at which they originated, to renew the conflict from which they proceeded, and with the help of propelling forces which at that time were not available to guide it towards a new solution. This revision of the process of repression can only partially be affected by means of the memory traces of the processes which led up to repression. The decisive part of the work is carried through by creating—in the relationship to the physician, in "the transference"—new editions of those early conflicts, in which the patient strives to behave as he originally behaved, while one calls upon all the available forces in his soul to bring him to another decision. The transference is thus the battlefield where all the contending forces must meet.

All the libido and the full strength of the opposition against it are concentrated upon the one thing, upon the relationship to the physician; thus it becomes inevitable that the symptoms should be deprived of their libido; in place of the patient's original illness appears the artificially-acquired transference, the transference disorder; in place of a variety of unreal objects of his libido appears the one object, also "phantastic", of the person of the physician. This new struggle which arises concerning this object is by means of the analyst's suggestions lifted to the surface, to the higher mental levels, and is there worked out as a normal mental conflict. Since a new repression is thus avoided, the opposition between the ego and the libido comes to an end; unity is restored within the patient's mind. When the libido has been detached from its temporary object in the person of the physician it cannot return to its earlier objects, but is at the disposal of the ego.

The therapeutic work thus falls into two phases; in the first all the libido is forced away from the symptoms into the transference and there concentrated; in the second the battle rages round this new object and the libido is made free from it. The change that is decisive for a successful outcome of this renewed conflict lies in the preclusion of repression, so that the libido cannot again withdraw itself from the ego by a flight into the unconscious. It is made possible by changes in the ego ensuing as a consequence of the analyst's suggestions. At the expense of the unconscious the ego becomes wider by the work of interpretation which brings the unconscious material into consciousness; through education it becomes reconciled to the libido and is made willing to grant it a certain degree of satisfaction; and its horror of the claims of its libido is lessened by the new capacity it acquires to expend a certain amount of the libido in sublimation. The more nearly the course of the treatment corresponds with this ideal description the greater will be the success of the psycho-analytic therapy.[1]

So far in this essay I have maintained the view put forward by Freud "that religious phenomena are to be understood only on the model of the neurotic symptoms of the individual, . . . as a return of long forgotten important happenings in the primeval history of the human race".[2] And it is of importance, as well as of interest, to observe how a difference of presupposition can alter the whole force of such a statement. Had it not been for human sin, it would have been unnecessary to worship God in the forms and ceremonies of human religion; and so in this way religion may justly be considered a symptom of human disease. Realizing, therefore, that to regard religious beliefs and practices in this way does not necessarily demolish the supernatural foundation of religion, we may justifiably ask whether or not any cure of the obsessive symptoms of religion is possible. Freud has, of course,

[1] *Introductory Lects.*, etc., pp. 380–1.
[2] *Moses and Monotheism*, p. 94.

suggested what he considers to be the destined fate of religious belief,[1] but I do not propose to discuss his opinions here, because I believe that the whole of the Freudian Theological argument—as distinct, that is, from the purely Psychological aspects of his work—is based on the presupposition that God does not exist. It would therefore be futile to attempt to counter such an argument, based as it is on a presupposition which is not only unacceptable, but which also could not legitimately be made by Freud while speaking simply as a scientist. If, however, any other criticism of the Freudian view is required, I would refer my readers to the last pages of Dr. William Brown's book *Psychology and Psycho-therapy*, in which we may read the following:

> Starting from science, we are ultimately forced to a new point of view, and find that a merely scientific point of view is not sufficient. Besides the scientific point of view, there is the point of view of the *value* of existence, which is the eternal aspect as contrasted with the merely temporal. A general philosophy of value is required to supplement and give meaning to the general system of scientific explanation of cosmic process. In other words, science needs to be supplemented by philosophy and religion.[2]

If now we compare with the condition of a person suffering from an obsessional neurosis the state of man afflicted, as it were, with a disease consisting of a multiplicity of religious ceremonies and beliefs of a compulsive character, which like the obsessive symptoms of a neurotic brought no lasting satisfaction or relief, we may legitimately suppose that if the former can be cured by Psycho-analysis, the latter may also be cured by some analogous process. In fact, we may hope to find that cure in Christianity, since we believe that to be a religion which so transcends all other religions as to be of a completely different quality—a belief that is clearly shown in the Epistle to the Hebrews, from which we have had occasion to quote already some words particularly appropriate in this connection.[3]

[1] Compare *The Future of an Illusion* and *Moses and Monotheism*, *passim*.　　　　[2] Op. cit., p. 202.　　　　[3] See p. 102, n. 2.

133

7. *Jesus Christ as the Analyst of the Soul*

If now we compare the work of Jesus Christ with that of the Psycho-analytic physician, we shall expect to find that his work will consist in bringing to the consciousness of man the repressed material which had been the cause of his religious neurosis. But immediately we find ourselves confronted by a difficulty. If Jesus was a true and normal man, how could he bring this repressed material to his own conscious mind, quite apart from doing the same for other people? That is to say, if we accept belief in the real humanity of Jesus Christ and in the universality of the effects of Adam's sin upon mankind, then it will appear that Jesus too must have shared in the universal repressions of mankind. In order to answer this problem I must refer to, and try to make clearer, what I have said earlier.

Saint Paul speaks of Christ as the second Adam and the new man, but also lays emphasis on the fact that he was born of a woman.[1] In this way we see what appear to be two incompatible characteristics in Christ's humanity—the sinlessness of Adam before the Fall, and the inherited sinfulness of mankind after the Fall. It may, of course, be argued that this paradox is to be resolved by the doctrine of the Immaculate Conception of the Blessed Virgin Mary. This, however, is no real solution, since it in reality only puts the problem as it were back a generation, and makes us ask two further questions: how was it that Mary could be truly conceived and born of human parents without sin? and, if Mary was thus miraculously sinless, why could not everyone else be so without the intervention of a divine Saviour? This doctrine must therefore, I feel, be dismissed, since not only is its only Scriptural authority founded upon a misinterpretation, but

[1] See 1 Corinthians, xv, 45, 47: "And so it is written, The first man Adam was made a living soul; the last Adam was made a quickening spirit ... The first man is of the earth earthy; the second man is the Lord from heaven"; and Galatians, iv, 4: "But when the fulness of the time was come, God sent forth his Son, made of a woman, made under the law ..."

it also raises problems as great as that which it purports to solve and thus confuses rather than clarifies the whole question.

There are two facts which must be taken into consideration in order to resolve the problem of the sinlessness and true humanity of Jesus Christ—first, the cause of the inherited sinfulness of man, and second, the Christian belief in the Virgin Birth of Jesus. Adam before the Fall was able to know God face to face in a manner which was impossible after sin had entered into the world. According to what has been said earlier, this means that, whereas before the Fall intercourse with God had been possible at a conscious level, after the Fall this was impossible and direct access to God ceased. The knowledge of God was repressed and God was forgotten; but this knowledge continued to exist in the unconscious system of humanity collectively, being held in repression by a resistance which gained its power from the strength of man's desires against God and his sense of guilt which had originally been the cause of the repression. And, we may add, it was because of being thus cut off from God that man continued to sin, since his access to the divine guidance through the human conscience was only vague and obscured. Jesus, therefore, being "made of a woman, made under the law",[1] inherited in his own unconscious system this knowledge of God. But for a complete understanding of the significance of this possession by Jesus *as a man* of the unconscious knowledge of God, we must also consider the nature of his conception and birth. In endeavouring earlier to trace the origin of sin in man, we put forward the suggestion that the desire of man for superiority over God, or for at least equality with him, found a means of expression in the sexual function. In this procreative act, which is shared by the male and the female, mankind appeared to achieve the objects of its desires —independence, through creative activity, and immortality, through the perpetuation of the species. If this is so, then we may recall Saint Augustine's views already mentioned, that it is by such repeated procreative acts that the blight of original sin is transmitted: or, in other words, that the sin

[1] Galatians, iv, 4.

135

of Adam created a predisposition to sin in the manner of that first sin—a permanent characteristic of subsequent generations who, when confronted by the same situation, reacted in the same way, it would, therefore, seem to follow from this that a man born of a woman without a previous act of parental sexual intercourse would not share in that inherited sinfulness, for in the absence of such a previous sexual union of a man and a woman the unconscious desire of man against God is denied a means of expression. Thus, if Jesus Christ was born of a Virgin, it would be possible for him to be conceived and born without his human parent sharing in the universal sin, because his birth had been accomplished without the apparently necessary intervention of a human father. Moreover, if we are to have a right view of the sinlessness of Mary, I believe that we are to see it in this limited sense of the sinless conception of Jesus—a conception, that is, without the universal sin on the part of Jesus' mother.[1] Indeed, by the very nature of Jesus' conception without the agency of a human father, the birth of Jesus must, for Mary, have been robbed of that form of parental pride which is the outward expression of the human revolt against God; and at the same time it would be free from any sense of guilt such as may attend any ordinary conception out of wedlock. On the contrary, the conception of Jesus was an act of submission to God on the part of Mary, such as no ordinary conception is.[2]

In order to avoid any possible misunderstanding on the subject of Jesus' true human descent and his sinlessness, these two points should also be taken into consideration.

[1] The later events of Mary's life seem to support this view. Had she been absolutely sinless, it is difficult to understand why she did not appreciate the significance of finding Jesus in the Temple among the doctors, or why later on she endeavoured to restrain our Lord from his preaching (see Luke, ii, 48–50; Mark, iii, 31–2). Further, it seems contrary to the plain meaning of the Scripture, if it is held that Mary's sinlessness was dependent on a perpetual virginity. Matthew, i, 25—"and (Joseph) knew her not till she had brought forth her firstborn son . . ."—seems to imply that Joseph knew Mary after Jesus' birth.

[2] See Luke ii, 38: And Mary said, Behold the handmaid of the Lord; be it unto me according to thy word.

Freud views the human race, taken as a whole, and its mental development as being parallel to the individual and his mental development. Just as a man grows up from childhood, repressing in that process of growth some of his infantile thoughts and desires, so also does the human race; though of the actual mechanism of this mental continuity he does not seem to give any account. The child is assumed to be born with a mental inheritance from his parents, in his unconscious system, which contains all their repressed thoughts. In such a manner was the repressed knowledge of God, together with our first ancestor's desires against his Creator, and the sense of guilt resulting from his primal sin, transmitted to later generations.

Now, I would suggest that in the case of mankind after Adam, the new sexual act, by which the next generation is produced, acts as a stimulus to these repressed concepts of desire and guilt which urges them to break from repression into consciousness; but they are thrust back again by the endopsychic censorship and so, in the adult, remain unconscious. In the new-born infant, of course, who, so far as can be seen, seems to be to a great measure free from the repressions of the adult, these inherited concepts may be at a conscious or preconscious level, only to be repressed later on in life. Thus, if only indirectly, it is the act of sexual intercourse on the part of the parents which accounts for the continued repression in the mind of the offspring of the desire and the sense of guilt which were respectively the cause and the result of Adam's sin.

On the other hand, even without any repetition of the sexual act, subsequent generations would inherit these repressions—but with a difference. If a person could be born without such an act of sexual intercourse on the part of his parents, then, although he would naturally inherit the content of his parent's unconscious, there would be no stimulus such as I have spoken of above, and the psychic censorship could, so to speak, be caught off its guard, as indeed happens partially in dreams. The desire and the sense of guilt, which were transmitted from the parent's unconscious, could remain at a conscious or preconscious level in the infant, or at any rate could become conscious in the adult, because the absence of the repeated (albeit unconsciously repeated) sin of Adam on the part of his parent would not be there, and would not therefore create, or recreate, that psychic barrier which normally represses such transmitted concepts. And this is what I have tried to suggest happened in the birth of Jesus Christ.[1]

From these observations the important fact emerges, that viewed as a man Jesus was like other men in that like them he possessed the fullness of human experience as it was transmitted to him through his Mother at an unconscious level; but was unlike other men in that the absence of parental sin in his conception and birth released him from the curse of original sin. In this way also the repression of the endopsychic censorship was dispelled, because his conception had been achieved without giving expression to man's sinful desires against God, and so Jesus could know consciously what other men could only know unconsciously. In him, therefore, we may see a man released from repression, and so possessing not only the knowledge of God consciously as Adam had done, but with it also, the knowledge of humanity's sinful desires and its sense of guilt.

Thus it would appear that the work of Jesus Christ upon earth might have been achieved simply by telling men of God's nature and of human sins—that is, by exposing what in fact lay buried in man's unconscious. Indeed, it may be suggested that the first part of Jesus' ministry, the preaching of repentance, was directed to this end. In actual practice, however, such a process could not achieve that end. As in Psycho-analytic therapy, it was not enough merely to inform men of their repressed thoughts, since what was told them would not replace those thoughts, but merely be accepted alongside of them. Nevertheless, this part of Jesus' ministry

[1] Such a view of the conscious knowledge of human sin by the sinless Jesus, through his sinless birth, seems to be in harmony with Saint Paul's words, "For he hath made him to be sin for us, who knew no sin"—2 Corinthians, v, 21.

—the revelation of the nature of God and of man's sin, or the revelation of the content of the unconscious—remains an essential part of the work of Jesus as the Saviour of mankind, though its aim could not be achieved without the other part of his work: his prophetic ministry could only be realized through his priestly and sacrificial ministry.

8. *The Transference of the Libido to Christ*

There are two features in the Gospels which at first sight may appear to have no real connection with one another. They are the demand upon the believer for love towards God and towards Jesus Christ; and our Lord's repeated warnings that in order to accomplish his work he must suffer and die. If, however, we are to regard Jesus as the divine Psychiatrist, the physician of the soul, then I would suggest that in these two contrary attitudes on the part of man towards him, we are to see the ambivalent manifestations of what has already been spoken of in describing individual Psycho-analytic therapy—namely, the Transference of the Libido. For convenience I shall endeavour to deal separately with these two phenomena, the love and the hatred of man for Jesus.

The prophetic ministry of Jesus may really be regarded as the preaching of repentance and of the need of love and faith towards God, or as the exposure of the content of the unconscious; and both of these amount to virtually the same thing, the restoration of the lost communion with and dependence on God. But as in the treatment of an individual neurosis, this object could only be achieved as a result of the Transference of the Libido; that is to say, man had to transfer to the person of Jesus the feelings of hatred and of love which he had in the infancy of the human race felt for God, and which in the perverted form of a desire for equality with God had been the cause of human sin. Thus in killing Jesus man repeated symbolically upon him the primal act of Adam's revolt against God, just as an individual transfers to the analyst his infantile feelings for his parents. But had Jesus been simply a man, like all other men, this act could not have had any therapeutic value; it is only because Jesus Christ was himself God, and is accepted as such by the Christian, that his death had any beneficial effect. Moreover, Jesus' death differed from the death of the symbolic victim of totemistic religion in this respect, that whereas the latter was an expression of unconscious desires directed against God, the former, the death of Christ, was an expression of a conscious desire directed against the person of Christ.

If we are correct in thus suggesting that the death of our Lord is a part of a therapeutic process analogous to the transference of hostile feelings on the part of a neurotic patient on to the person of the physician, then the need for love towards Jesus may be regarded as a more positive form of the Transference. The sense of love for God, which was part of that communion with his Creator enjoyed by Adam before the Fall, and which must have been repressed as an integral part of the knowledge of God, is also transferred to the person of Christ as the physician of the soul. We may then see both in the hostility and the love of man towards Jesus a transference of those feelings which man had for God in the infancy of the human race: viewed psychologically we may see in them a manifestation of the transference of the Libido which found a necessary part of the Psycho-analytic therapy. "Thus it is written," we may say, "and thus it behoved Christ to suffer," [1] as a part of his work of salvation as inevitable and as necessary as the love which the believer, the "patient", must show for him. If then such a view is not mistaken, that the passion and death of Christ were a working out upon him of the trans-

[1] Luke, xxiv, 46; and compare John, xi, 49–52: "And one of them, named Caiaphas, being the high priest that same year, said unto them, Ye know nothing at all, nor consider that it is expedient for us, that one man should die for the people, and that the whole nation perish not. And this spake he not of himself: but being high priest that year, he prophesied that Jesus should die for that nation; and not for that nation only, but that also he should gather together in one the children of God that were scattered abroad"; and xix, 10–11: "Then saith Pilate unto him, Speakest thou not unto me? Knowest thou not that I have power to crucify thee, and have power to release thee? Jesus answered, Thou couldest have no power at all against me except it were given thee from above."

ferred unconscious feelings of man towards God, we may perhaps be able more fully to understand why it was that the Saviour of mankind had to be both loved and hated by those to whom he came to reveal the true nature of God. Thus it was that the suffering servant of God was able to pass on to men the knowledge of God, which he himself possessed, by his suffering.[1]

But it must be remembered that if Jesus is to be regarded thus as the great psychiatrist, then the love which is shown by the disciple towards Jesus is not the end of the treatment but only the means to that end. As Freud points out, the Transference—that is, the artificial relationship set up between the patient and the physician—has to be resolved, and the libido must be "sublimated", that is, directed into other less selfish and more social channels. This process of sublimation Freud regards as a diversion of sexual energy into channels of expression which are asexual. Such a view of the finding of redirected sexual energy in such things as Art or Music, or even in philanthropic works, depends entirely on the Freudian theory that the sexual is the dominant instinct, and that other forms of psychical energy—of libido, in the wider sense in which it is used by Jung[2] or of Bergson's *élan vital*—are in fact sexual in origin, though not in aim and direction. I cannot, however, help but think that Jung's theory represents a more accurate picture, and that his term "transformation" of the libido[3] probably gives a better idea of the conversion of psychical energy from one object to another than does "sublimation" which implies the primacy of the sexual instinct. The difference between these views may perhaps be shown by means of the diagrams on the next page, in which L represents libido, S the sexual instinct, and ABCD other expressions of psychical energy. In (1), the Freudian view, S is equivalent to L, and ABCD are sublimations of S;

---

[1] Compare Isaiah, liii, 4–11, and especially, "by his knowledge shall my righteous servant justify many; for he shall bear their iniquities."

[2] See *Contributions to Analytical Psychology*, p. 32.

[3] *Psychology of the Unconscious*, pp. 87 ff.

in (2), which represents Jung's theory, SABCD are all different ways of expressing L. Even if, as in (3), S is the strongest and most dominant expression of L, so that the energy belonging properly to ABCD is diverted to S, this does not mean that if the Libido is diverted back again to ABCD they are expressions of S.

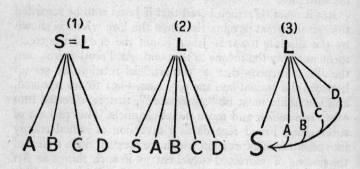

It would follow from what has been said earlier that a major part of man's psychical energy, or libido, has been absorbed in the unconscious conflict which resulted from man's sin against God. When, therefore, we say that man's desires against God found a means of expression in the exercise of sexuality, this does not mean that those desires were of a sexual character; and so also, when we come to speak here of the redirection of psychical energy, we must regard it as a transformation of libido, rather than as a sublimation of it. Thus love for God is not to be regarded as a sublimation of sexual desire, any more than sexual love is a sublimation of love for God; both are different expressions, with different objects in view, of an asexual libido. With this distinction in mind we may now return to the subject of man's relations to Jesus and to God which result from Jesus' work in the world. We must, therefore, distinguish between love for Jesus, which is a manifestation of the Transference, and love for God and for one's neighbours, which is to be regarded as a transformation (an apparent sublimation) of the libido, and a restoration of the relationship with God and mankind which would have existed but for human sin.[1] This distinction is perhaps difficult to comprehend, since our love for God must include love for Christ as God, and also since in the course of the soul's cure a partial transformation of libido must show itself before the Transference is completely resolved. We have, indeed, as members of the human race generally, been saved by Jesus Christ, but individually we are in the process of being saved: paradoxically, it may seem, we are σεσωσμένοι and at the same time σωζόμενοι, inasmuch as we are in process of appropriating and assimilating the benefits of Christ's completed work.

Further, if we observe carefully this difference between the love of Jesus as the means of salvation and the love of God as its end, we shall not fall into the error of Freud, when he speaks of Christianity as the final overthrowing and defeat of the Father, and of the Son "becoming God himself beside the Father and in truth in place of the Father"; and when he goes on to elaborate thus: "Originally a Father religion, Christianity became a Son religion. The fate of having to displace the Father it could not escape."[2] I should like to point out also that such a misconception of the relative position of the Son and the Father, which terms are, after all, only analogies from human relationships, is a very real danger in the teaching of children about the love of Jesus. Not only does it breed a sentimental attitude to religion, but it tends to ignore the fact that the primary object of Christ's work, as of the Christian Faith, is the reconciliation of God's

---

[1] Compare John, xxi, 15–17, and xiv, 15, with xiii, 34–5: "So when they had dined, Jesus saith to Simon Peter, Simon, son of Jonas, lovest thou me more than these? He saith unto him, Yea, Lord; thou knowest that I love thee. He saith unto him, Feed my lambs, etc." This we may compare with: "If ye love me, keep my commandments"; and "A new commandment I give unto thee, That ye love one another; as I have loved you, that ye also love one another. By this shall all men know that ye are my disciples, if ye have love one to another." Love of Jesus is to be expressed in love for one's fellows.

[2] *Moses and Monotheism*, pp. 214–15.

rebellious children to their heavenly Father.[1] Such an error is clearly repudiated in the New Testament, as, for example, by Saint Paul when he says: "Then cometh the end when he (Jesus) shall have delivered up the Kingdom to God, even the Father; when he shall have put down all rule and all authority and power."[2] This too is implied by Saint John, who puts these words into the mouth of Jesus: "He that believeth on me, believeth not on me, but on him that sent me."[3]

There is, however, another side to the picture which we have tried to give here of the meaning of the sufferings of Christ. In speaking of the original religious neurosis, Totemism, I endeavoured to show how the victim of the sacrifice was the symbolic representative of the God and also, at the same time, of the common worshipper. We have also seen that the artificially created neurosis, which occurs in patients undergoing Psycho-analytic treatment, reproduces the outward symbolic forms of the symptoms of the original neurosis; but that it invests these symptoms with a new meaning. Thus the death of Jesus may be expected to represent the symbolic death of the totem-animal in both the senses which we have traced in Totemism, that is, as both positive and negative expressions of man's unconscious desires. Not only does man transfer to the person of Jesus his wishes against God, but also his own desire for self-punishment; so that Jesus, whom we believe to be not only God but also man, is in this latter capacity the representative of man, and suffers on account of human sin as substitute for guilty humanity.[4]

[1] Compare 2 Corinthians, v, 18–19: "And all things are of God, who hath reconciled us to himself by Jesus Christ, and hath given to us the ministry of reconciliation; to wit, that God was in Christ, reconciling the world unto himself, not imputing their trespasses unto them; and hath committed unto us the word of reconciliation."

[2] 1 Corinthians, xv, 24.   [3] John, xii, 44.

[4] Compare, for example, 2 Corinthians, v, 21: "For he made him to be sin for us, who knew no sin." 1 Peter, iii, 18: "For Christ also hath once suffered for sins, the just for the unjust, that he might bring us to God . . ." And also Romans, v, 6; 1 Corinthians, xv, 3, etc.

Moreover, as the purpose of the work of Jesus Christ was the restoration of the lost communion with God the Father, and so too the conquest of the fear of death, which had been the inevitable result of man's sin—we might almost call it a "mortality-phobia"—the Resurrection and Ascension of Jesus have a double significance, similar to that of his death. Not only are they the outward proof of the divinity of Jesus and the truth of his teaching, but also they are signs of the absolute immortality of God (in so far as Jesus Christ as God could not be killed), and thus of the impossibility of man's desires against God, and (in so far as Jesus Christ as man was truly dead and raised from death) the sign of the restoration of the lost communion with God, achieved by the man Jesus through his voluntary acceptance on behalf of man of the punishment unconsciously desired by mankind for itself.

In giving this brief interpretation of the work of Christ as our Saviour, I have made no attempt to explain—or should I say, "to explain away"?—the Christian belief in the Incarnation, the Virgin Birth, or the Resurrection of Christ, because I believe them to be essential, and not impossible, parts of the Christian Faith, which are also, incidentally, necessary for the interpretation I have tried to give. Furthermore, as an interpretation, it is not a definition of Christology in the sense in which the Nicene Creed or the Quicunque Vult are attempts to define Christ's manhood and divinity; but it is only an attempt to explain the relevance and significance of Christ's nature in relation to his work as the physician of man's soul. If the reader is willing to accept the one absolute pre-supposition—belief in the existence of God—which underlies the whole of the argument I have tried to set out, then such beliefs need no such explanation any more than life and existence do, since they are no more supernatural or extraordinary than what through familiarity with the mechanics of life we recognize as ordinary and natural parts of God's creation. Indeed, if we believe in God, the term "supernatural" loses its real force, for the whole of natural life is in a sense supernatural inasmuch as it depends upon the existence of God before it could itself exist. If, therefore, we believe in God, it appears to be an idle question to ask if Christ could perform his miracles or be raised from the dead —as idle, indeed, as to ask whether or not man and the world in which we live have any existence apart from our own imagination.

9. *The Way of Salvation: The Sacraments as Symptoms of the Transference Disorder*

There remains now only one question to be answered— namely, how the individual is to appropriate and assimilate what Jesus Christ has done for the world; in other words, what is the process of individual salvation. In this process of the therapy of the soul, it is perhaps impossible to over- estimate the importance of faith in Jesus for the success of the "cure"; such faith in Jesus Christ as Saviour is propor- tionately as important for the individual seeking salvation from sin, as it is for the individual seeking a cure of an obsessive neurotic disease at the hands of a Psycho-analyst to have faith and confidence in the physician. And so of this, perhaps, I need say no more.

If we are correct in having pressed the analogy between Psycho-analysis and Religion so far, and in seeing the hatred and the love of man for Jesus Christ as manifestations of the Transference, then we must be prepared to come at this stage to a rather startling conclusion—that our own appropri- ation of the benefits of Christ's passion and death, or in other words the cure of our own souls, must take place by means of an artificially created neurosis, the transference disorder, which is a therapeutic process similar in outward form to, but in fact replacing, the old religious neurosis based on the unconscious desires of man directed against God. The symptoms of this fresh neurosis are, indeed, none other than the rites and ceremonies of the Christian Church, and their meaning, in relation to Jesus Christ, is parallel to the similar rites and ceremonies of Totemism in relation to God the Father. According to such a view, therefore, there is a very real and important difference between what otherwise appear to be almost identical phenomena: the ceremonies and taboos of Totemism are the outward signs of the disease of the human soul; the sacraments and beliefs of Christianity are the means whereby that disease is cured. If we are careful to draw clearly this distinction, which depends wholly on belief in the historic reality of the Incarnate Son of God, then we shall be able to see the real difference between heathen and Christian religion in spite of their apparent similarity. Also, if we are prepared to regard in this manner the Christian Sacraments as forms of the therapeutic transference-disorder, we shall see that they have only a temporary purpose, which will be fulfilled when to all mankind is restored the lost communion with God. This transitory character is, indeed, shown in the thought of Saint Paul, who speaks of the Eucharist in these words: "For as often as ye eat this bread, and drink this cup, ye do shew the Lord's death, *till he come.*" [1]

The two sacraments of the Christian religion, which are defined in the Book of Common Prayer as being "generally necessary to salvation"—namely, Baptism and the Holy Communion—are, as I have already indicated, to be understood as manifestations of the acquired transference-disorder, and are thus the means by which man arrives at that state of suggestibility which will enable him to receive and carry out the teaching of Jesus to love God and his fellow men. We shall not, therefore, be surprised to see that, according to such an interpretation, these sacraments have a symbolic meaning in relation to the person of Jesus Christ which is to be understood on the basis of the unconscious meaning of the quasi-sacramental ritual of Totemism in relation to the Totem-God. It is not, therefore, necessary to speak at great length about the symptomatic meaning of the sacraments, as the parallelism of them with Totemistic ceremonies is in many respects all too obvious.

To understand the psychological significance of Baptism as a part of the therapeutic process, there are three things which must be taken into consideration: the effects upon the believer

[1] 1 Corinthians, xi, 26.

which it is believed to bring about, the parallel forms of ceremony in the original religion-neurosis which it replaces, and the transference relationship of the believer to Jesus Christ. In Baptism, the baptized person, that is, if we like, the patient, becomes "a member of Christ, the child of God, and an inheritor of the Kingdom of Heaven". In Theodor Reik's essay on the "Puberty Rites of Savages,"[1] which are explained and interpreted by the Psycho-analytic method, the author comes to the conclusion that in them we are to see a symbolic attempt to break the incestuous attachment of the young savage to his mother, and to restore the bond of affection and loyalty to the father. Such an interpretation of an ostensibly religious ceremony only holds good so long as it is founded upon the Freudian theory that the origin of religion and morality are to be traced back to a purely human cause, namely to the incestuous desires of the sons for their mothers, and to the murder of the father of the primitive horde. If, however, such events as Freud describes as taking place in humanity's remote prehistory are at most, as I have suggested, only the immediate cause of the outbreak of a religious neurosis whose ultimate origin lies in man's repressed knowledge of God and his unconscious desires against God, and if, therefore, in these puberty rites we are to see the symbolic restoration of man's lost relationship not with his human father but with God, then in Baptism we may see the same end accomplished, and a similar symbolism employed. Like the symbolic death and resurrection of the savage initiate, which found a later expression also in the initiation rites of the mystery cults, the believer is baptized into the death of Christ;[2] and as a result of this identification with the sufferings of his representative, and the accompanying confession of guilt and of sin against God, he is delivered from the power of death and restored to sonship of God the Father.[3] So too

[1] *Ritual*, pp. 91 ff.

[2] Compare Romans, vi, 3: "Know ye not, that so many of us as were baptized into Jesus Christ were baptized into his death?"

[3] Compare Romans, vi, 8: "Now if we be dead with Christ, we believe that we shall also live with him."

Baptism into the death of Christ as the representative of man is a replacement of the rite of circumcision which, as part of the savage puberty rites, we have seen to be a symptomatic expression of the psychological need for the punishment of man's sin against God. Further, as the savage is separated from his mother and reborn as a member of the father group, so too the candidate at Baptism is purified from his sinful desires against God, which we have seen earlier to be symbolized by the incestuous desires towards the mother, and is restored to fellowship with God by a rebirth of water and the Spirit. Here as well we may trace an identification on the part of the believer with the person of Jesus Christ: the new birth of the Spirit in Baptism is a birth freed from the sexual-aggressive sin of ordinary conception and birth. Like Jesus, who was born of a virgin by the operation of the Spirit, and was then without sin, so also the Christian is born again and becomes the son of God and a member of Christ by virtue of this identification and by the operation of the same Spirit.[1]

Furthermore, if we were correct in our speculation earlier as to one of the possible meanings of the rite of circumcision as an outward sign of the desire for immortality, then we may also regard Baptism, which in Christianity quickly replaced circumcision as the initiation rite, as a symptomatic manifestation of a similar desire for the eternal life of God. Inheritance of eternal life is one of the gifts conferred by Baptism, and it may not be too fanciful to see in this idea of Baptism, as a means of procuring the desired gift of immortality, an unconscious repetition of a primitive ritual, which had associated the renewal of life with the shedding of the skin and a voyage by boat or a bathe in the water. The justification for this view is briefly as follows: If, as is generally acknowledged, the myths of the ancient gods and heroes reflect the ritual practices of bygone ages, then perhaps some of the myths concerning the loss of man's immortality also reflect the practices of an initiation rite. In these myths the coveted gift is sometimes obtained as a result of bathing or swimming in

[1] Compare John, iii, 3–8.

water, sometimes after a voyage in a boat.[1] Now as baptism commonly forms a part of many initiation and puberty rites, it may well be that this primitive washing was intended, like the rite of circumcision, to convey the gift of immortality. If this is so, there again we see that the myth reveals man's desire, and that both are reflected in the rite. In Christian Baptism the desire for immortality is expressed in the old ritual, but as a result of the transference of the libido its emphasis is now centred upon the person of Jesus Christ: even the myths which underlay the heathen ritual have their counterpart in the baptism of Jesus by John, for though the latter is an historical event, it has the same symbolic character as a myth.

So too the story of the Deluge, in which Noah and his family found safety by taking refuge in the ark, seems remarkably similar in certain respects to some of the Fall myths recorded by Frazer and referred to already. Noah retains his life by being in the ark, while, in some of the myths of the Fall, man gains eternal life by a voyage in a boat, though he subsequently forfeits it. Perhaps the story of Noah reflects an early ritual consisting of a voyage by boat, which had a similar purpose to baptism, namely the renewal of life. Certainly this parallelism between Baptism and Noah's stay in the ark is recognized quite early in Christian thought.[2]

Thus we may see that the Christian sacrament of Baptism is, as a result of the transference of the libido to Jesus, the successor to and replacement of, the primitive initiation ceremonies of our heathen ancestors; and that like them this rite is believed to confer membership of the divinity; a

[1] See Frazer: *Folk-Lore in the Old Testament* (Abridged Edition), pp. 27–9.

[2] See 1 Peter, iii, 20–1: " . . . in the days of Noah, while the ark was a preparing, wherein few, that is eight souls, were saved by water. The like figure whereunto even baptism doth also now save us . . . by the resurrection of Jesus Christ." Compare also the Prayer in the Order of Infant Baptism: "Almighty and everlasting God, who of thy great mercy didst save Noah and his family from perishing by water . . . look upon this child . . . that he . . . may be received into the ark of Christ's Church."

restoration of sonship to God by a new and spiritual birth; a cleansing from guilt by submission to a symbolic death; and the gift of immortality by a symbolic resurrection.

In the same way as we have considered the Sacrament of Baptism, we are now to consider the Holy Communion in relation to its believed effects upon the participant, its apparent parallels in Totemism, and its symbolic representation of the sufferings of Christ. We have already seen how the quasi-sacramental meals of the primitive worshipper of the totem-god were both positive and negative expressions of man's repressed desires towards God, and of his repressed sense of guilt towards God. So also in the sacrament of the Body and Blood of Christ, we are, I believe, to see the expression of such desires transferred to the person of Jesus Christ. To realize the full meaning of this, we must appreciate the psychological significance of remembrance, so as to understand what is meant by our Lord's words at the Last Supper when he instituted the Holy Eucharist: "This is my body which is given for you: this do in remembrance of me."[1] This idea of remembrance is also found in the thought of Saint Paul, who speaks of the Eucharist as showing forth the Lord's death[2] and it is echoed in the Prayer of Consecration and in the words of Administration in the Prayer Book Order of the Ministration of the Holy Communion. I do not intend here to discuss the relative merits or demerits of the ideas of the Eucharistic sacrifice which have given rise to the view that it is a repetition of the sacrifice of Calvary; all I would do is to point out that in *remembering* the death of Jesus we are in a real sense *repeating* it, by virtue of the very process of remembering. For in bringing any past experience into consciousness, by what we call "remembering" it, as distinct, that is, from being told about it, we do in fact re-live that experience mentally, and feel in remembrance the same

[1] Luke, xxii, 19: τοῦτο ποιεῖτε εἰς τὴν ἐμὴν ἀνάμνησιν. The word ἀνάμνησις in this context suggests that the repetition of the symbolic Eucharistic act is the stimulus, which causes the return to consciousness of the unconscious desires of man against God.

[2] 1 Corinthians, xi, 26.

emotions, as joy, sorrow, anger, which we felt when the remembered experience actually took place. Perhaps a little simple psychological insight would have spared the Church much of the controversy which has raged concerning this aspect of the nature of the Eucharistic sacrifice. However, I think we must recognize this fact, that in remembering the death of Christ in the Holy Communion we are repeating that death both mentally and symbolically. If we may thus see a continual repetition of the sacrifice of Christ in the Eucharistic sacrifice, then the parallelism of the symptoms of the transference disorder with the symptoms of the original neurosis show up more clearly.

If we consider first the positive expression of man's desires in the killing and eating of the totem animal, which symbolize the overcoming of God and the appropriation of his qualities of independence and immortality, then in the Eucharist we may see an expression of these same desires against God transferred to the person of Christ who is symbolically killed and eaten under the form of bread and wine, as God was killed and eaten under the form of the totem-animal. Here, as is the case in the transference-disorder of an individual, the same symbolic acts, the symptoms of the original neurosis, are invested with a new meaning, which is in this case transferred from God the Father to Jesus in his role of physician of the soul. In a similar way, the Eucharistic offering of the body and the blood of Christ may be regarded as a repetition of the substitutionary offering of Christ as man's representative upon the Cross. I have endeavoured to point out earlier how the totem-animal is the representative not only of God but also of man, and how its death is a negative expression of man's wishes against God, in the form of a desire and need for self-punishment. So too in the Eucharistic offering of Christ we are offering ourselves symbolically through a representative, and in so doing are satisfying through Christ our own previously unconscious desire for punishment, which through the acknowledgment of sin becomes a conscious feeling of guilt.

Another aspect of the Holy Communion which reproduces

in the transference-disorder the symptoms of the original neurosis is the idea of communion itself; that is, the idea that all the worshippers, by sharing in the communal act of breaking and eating the bread, share among themselves not only the benefits of the consumption of Christ's body and blood, but also the sense of guilt at the death of the divine victim.

We have already had occasion to notice that Saint Paul speaks of the transitory character of Christian Eucharistic worship, or, in other words, of the temporary nature of the transference-disorder.[1] In the following verses of the same chapter the Apostle goes on to speak of eating and drinking unworthily.[2] What has been said above may help to throw some light on this. Earlier in the same Epistle Saint Paul had drawn a distinction between being "partakers of the Lord's table, and of the table of devils",[3] or, according to a psychological interpretation, between the symptoms of the transference-disorder and the symptoms of the neurosis itself. A confusion of this kind is, indeed, very easily made, especially between Christianity and the more refined forms of Totemism, the mystery cults, which flourished in St. Paul's time. It was, therefore, most necessary for his Corinthian converts to be careful to distinguish between the two—to discern the Lord's body—and so to avoid a mere substitution, without any therapeutic value, of one neurosis for another. If the so-called believer thus confuses the Christian Eucharist with the sacrifice of heathenism, he will have degraded Christianity to the level of the spiritual disease for which he was trying to find a cure, and will indeed thus be eating and drinking damnation to himself.

In the view of the Sacraments of Baptism and the Holy

[1] 1 Corinthians, xi, 26: "For as often as ye eat this bread and drink this cup, ye do show the Lord's death *till he come.*"
[2] 1 Corinthians, xi, 27–9: "Wherefore whosoever shall eat this bread, and drink this cup of the Lord, unworthily, shall be guilty of the body and blood of the Lord . . . For he that eateth and drinketh unworthily, eateth and drinketh damnation to himself, not discerning the Lord's body."
[3] 1 Corinthians, x, 21.

Communion, which I have outlined briefly here, I have tried to show how, on the analogy of the transference-disorder in the Psycho-analytic treatment of individuals, the benefits of the passion and death of our Lord Jesus Christ may be appropriated by the believer. Further than this in our present state we cannot go, and so it is at this point that our study must draw to an end. For the completion of the Saviour's work, the complete resolution of the Transference, belongs to that higher world where we shall know even as also we are known, where the glorious majesty of God shall be revealed to all mankind and we can see our Father and Creator face to face. Here, however, like Moses upon the summit of Pisgah viewing the promised land which he could not himself enter, we can but look forward to that time when Christ shall have delivered up the kingdom unto God, and when the worship of God under forms and symbols shall be no longer needed. "And I John saw the holy city, new Jerusalem . . . and I saw no temple therein; for the Lord God Almighty and the Lamb are the temple of it."[1]

---

[1] Revelations, xxi, 2, 22.

CONCLUSION

THE course of the argument in the foregoing pages may appear to have led us far from our original goal to a new and, as it may seem to some, a rather fanciful interpretation of the Christian religion. Such an interpretation, however, was in a sense inevitable once we began to apply the Psycho-analytic method to the examination of religion while still affirming the truth of the existence of God. But it may be objected that an interpretation of this kind cannot bear close scrutiny, on the grounds that it depends on anthropological and psychological theories which are, in the light of more recent research, now untenable.

This objection, however, though it is undoubtedly valid as a criticism of Freud, does not, I would submit, carry the same weight it would seem to as a criticism of the present essay. It was my primary purpose, as was stated in the preface, to use, rather than to criticize, the theories of Freud, with a limited objective in view—that of showing that, even when examined by the Psycho-analytic method, the phenomena of religious beliefs and practices are not incompatible with belief in the existence of God, but are patient of a theistic interpretation. To do this it was necessary to accept much that today may appear unacceptable, in the light of the advances which have been made in the study of both psychology and anthropology: and I have, therefore, accepted what appear to be rather dubious theories simply for the sake of argument.

Although Freud's theories may now be considered out of date, there are two observations which I feel deserve consideration. First, that they may not be so much out of date as out of fashion. Much that Freud has put forward cannot be proved or disapproved by ordinary methods of argument, for many of his theories are not in the strict sense scientific theories but rather philosophical propositions, and the evidence required for proving or disproving them does not really exist. His theories and speculations are suspect because they are unpalatable: because they are not acceptable they are not accepted. The second observation is this: that while there are many who disagree with Freud's theories, there are still some who accept them, and it is to those who may have been influenced by Freud and his disciples that this essay is addressed. If such people have swallowed Freud's theories, both psychological and anthropological, then I would submit it would be futile to argue against the grounds on which those theories are based—to argue, that is, against the psychological and anthropological bases of Freud's philosophy. The method I have adopted has, therefore, intentionally ignored to a large extent the arguments brought against Freud by more modern psychologists and anthropologists. So that if this essay, which is submitted as nothing more than an *argumentum ad hominem*, and not as an interpretation of religion of universal validity, is criticized on the grounds that, for example, its anthropological data are inaccurate, this must be regarded not as a criticism of this essay, but as a criticism of Freud.

Why then, it may be asked, have I endeavoured to produce an argument resting on such doubtful foundations? There are two ways in which a military campaign may be conducted, and these may serve as an analogy to illustrate the principles on which I have tried to attack Freud. The enemy's line of battle may be attacked on a broad front, with the object simply of driving the enemy further and further back; such a method is a slow and expensive one, and will rarely succeed in breaking the enemy's front. The other method, that of the Blitzkrieg, is to fling all one's available resources against a comparatively narrow sector of the front, in order to pierce the enemy's line and thus destroy his whole battle order. As an analogy, of course, this is not wholly adequate, but it will serve our purpose. The usual method of attacking any theory like that of Freud is to attack it on a broad front: that is, to attack each individual part of the theory and to endeavour, in what proves often to be a series of protracted and inconclusive engagements, to disprove those parts severally. The other

156

method is that which I have adopted—namely, to limit the scope of the attack to what seemed the most vulnerable point of his whole system; that is to say, the question of belief in the existence of God. And in so doing I have intentionally ignored and refrained from attacking the other parts of the front.

It is not for me to say whether or not this attack has succeeded: but it should be remembered that its objective was a limited one. In conclusion, therefore, I may perhaps be permitted to indicate once more that my purpose in writing this was to show that the presuppositions of Freud determine from the very outset the conclusions of his arguments on the nature of belief in God, and that the Psycho-analytic method in itself proves nothing. The answer to the question of the existence or non-existence of God, of the reality or unreality of the supernatural, belongs not to the realm of science but rather to that of metaphysics. It is for others to judge of my success or failure in this endeavour to transfer the controversy to its proper sphere.